JAGUAR

4·2 'E' TYPE AND 2+2

CW00763586

OPERATING, MAINTENANCE
AND SERVICE HANDBOOK

JAGUAR CARS LIMITED, COVENTRY, ENGLAND

Telephone	Code	Telegraphic Address
ALLESLEY 2121	BENTLEYS SECOND	"JAGUAR," COVENTRY. Telex 31622

Publication No. E/131/6.

FOREWORD

This Handbook gives the information necessary for the satisfactory operation and maintenance of the Jaguar 4·2 " E " Type and 2 + 2.

Major service operations and repairs are not described and the owner is recommended to have operations not covered in this handbook executed by the local Jaguar Distributor or Dealer, who is in a position to give authoritative advice and service. The satisfactory running and fine performance of which the car is capable, depends to a great extent upon the care and attention which it receives from the owner. We, therefore, earnestly recommend that careful attention is paid to the following instructions and that the servicing detailed in the " Routine Maintenance " section is carried out at the suggested periods. The text of the handbook is divided into three main sections :—

Operating Instructions

deals with the operation of the controls and equipment.

Routine Maintenance

deals with the maintenance of the various components of the car at certain mileage intervals.

Service Instructions

deals with certain operations which should normally be undertaken by a Jaguar Distributor or Dealer, but which are included as a guide for the enthusiast or the owner living in a remote district.

Note

All references in this handbook to " right-hand side " and " left-hand side " are made assuming the person to be looking from the rear of the car or unit.

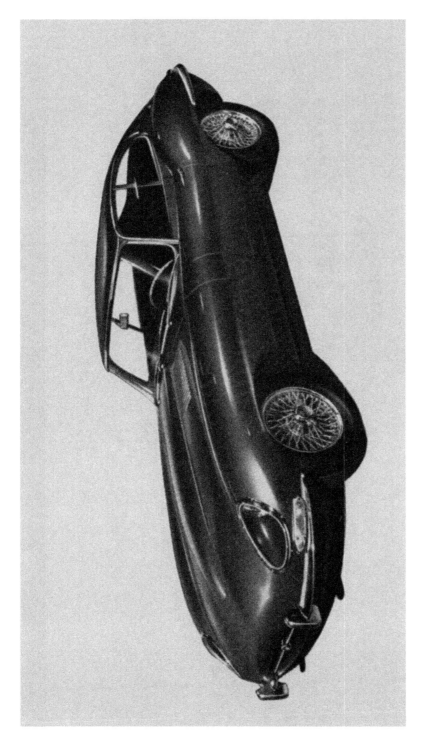

The 4·2 "E" Type Fixed Head Coupe (Hardtop)

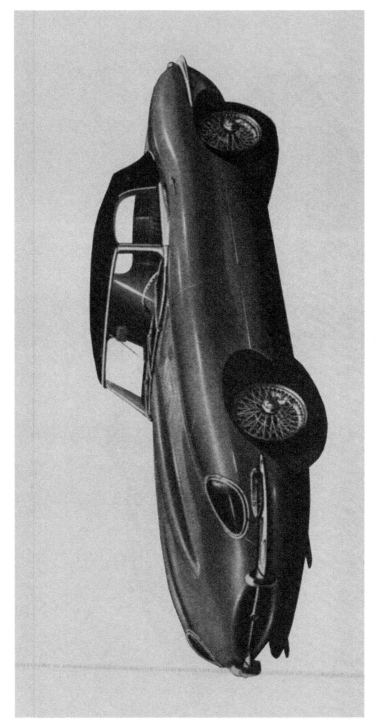

The 4·2 "E" Type Open 2-Seater (Roadster)

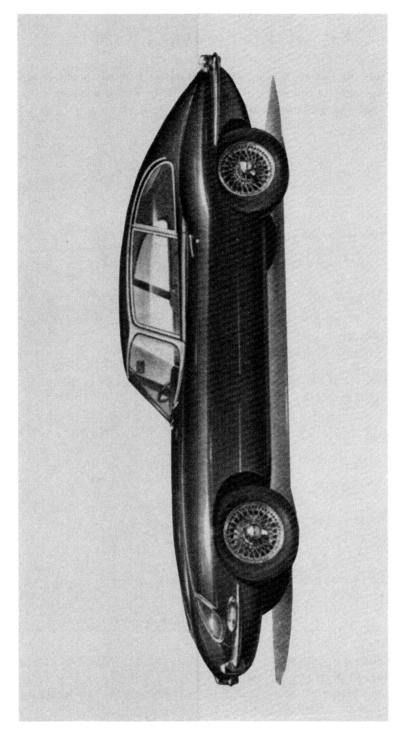

THE 4.2 'E' TYPE 2 + 2

CAR IDENTIFICATION

It is imperative that the Car and Engine numbers, together with any prefix or suffix letters are quoted in any correspondence concerning this vehicle. If the unit in question is the Gearbox the Gearbox number and any prefix or suffix letters must also be quoted. This also applies when ordering spare parts.

Car Number

Stamped on the right-hand frame cross member above the hydraulic damper mounting.

Engine Number

Stamped on the right-hand side of the cylinder block above the oil filter and at the front of the cylinder head casting.

/8 or /9 following the engine number denotes the compression ratio.

Gearbox Number

Stamped on a shoulder at the left-hand rear corner of the gearbox casing and on the top cover.

Automatic Transmission

Stamped on a plate attached to the Unit.

Body Number

Stamped on a plate attached to the right-hand side of the scuttle.

Key Numbers

The keys provided operate the ignition switch and door locks.

Fig. 1. *The identification numbers are also stamped on the plate indicated.*

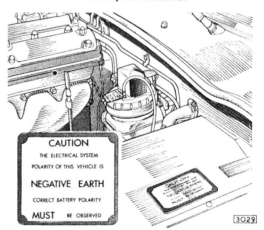

CAUTION

THE ELECTRICAL SYSTEM POLARITY OF THIS VEHICLE IS

NEGATIVE EARTH

CORRECT BATTERY POLARITY

MUST BE OBSERVED

IMPORTANT

These cars have Negative Earth (ground) systems and certain of the electrical components are different to those fitted to positive earth cars.

When fitting auxiliary equipment or replacing any of the electrical components use only those specified for this particular model.

INDEX

7

INDEX

GENERAL DATA

Engine

Number of cylinders	6
Bore	3.625″ (92·07 mm.)
Stroke	4.1732″ (106 mm.)
Cubic Capacity	4,235 c.c. (258.43 cu. ins.)
Compression ratio	8 to 1 or 9 to 1
Distributor contact breaker gap	.014″—.016″ (.36—.41 mm.)
Sparking Plug Type	
8 to 1 and 9 to 1 comp. ratio	Champion N.11Y
Sparking plug gap	.025″ (.64 mm.)
Ignition timing	
8 to 1 comp. ratio	9° B.T.D.C.
9 to 1 comp. ratio	10° B.T.D.C.

Valve Clearances (cold)	Inlet	Exhaust
Normal Touring	.004″ (.10 mm.)	.006″ (.15 mm.)
Racing	.006″ (.15 mm.)	.010″ (.25 mm.)

Valve Seat Angle	
Inlet and Exhaust	45°
Firing Order	1, 5, 3, 6, 2, 4

Tightening Torque Figures

Flywheel	67 lbs. ft. (9.2 kg. m.)
Connecting rod	37 lbs. ft. (5.1 kg. m.)
Main bearings	83 lbs. ft. (11.5 kg. m.)
Cylinder head	58 lbs. ft. (8.0 kg. m.)
Camshaft bearings	15 lbs. ft. (2.0 kg. m.)

Carburetters

Type : S.U. H.D.8 (triple)

Gearbox

Type : Four speed—synchromesh on 1st, 2nd, 3rd and top.

Type : Model 8 Automatic Transmission (2 + 2 only).

Front Suspension and Steering

Castor angle	$2° \pm \frac{1}{2}°$ positive
Camber angle	$\frac{1}{4}° \pm \frac{1}{2}°$ positive
Front wheel alignment	$\frac{1}{16}″$—$\frac{1}{8}″$ (1.6—3.2 mm.) toe-in

Rear Suspension

Camber angle .... $\frac{3}{4}° \pm \frac{1}{4}°$ negative

Final Drive

Type : Hypoid, semi-floating.

Ratios		
U.S.A., Canada and Newfoundland	3.54 : 1
All other countries	3.07 : 1
Automatic Transmission (2 + 2 only, U.S.A. and Canada)	3.31 : 1
Automatic Transmission (2 + 2 only, All other countries)	2.88 : 1

Tyres

MINIMUM TYRE PRESSURES (checked with tyres COLD)

Dunlop Road Speed RS5. 6.40 x 15.	**Front**	**Rear**
For speeds up to 130 mph (210 kph)	23 lb./sq. in. (1.62 kg./sq. cm.)	25 lb./sq. in. (1.76 kg./sq. cm.)
For speeds up to maximum	30 lb./sq. in. (2.11 kg./sq. cm.)	35 lb./sq. in. (2.46 kg./sq. cm.)
Dunlop SP 41.HR. 185 x 15.		
For speeds up to 125 mph (200 kph)	32 lb./sq. in. (2.25 kg./sq. cm.)	32 lb./sq. in. (2.25 lb./sq. cm.)
For speeds up to maximum	40 lb./sq. in. (2.81 kg./sq. cm.)	40 lb./sq. in. (2.81 kg./sq. cm.)

NOTE. The Dunlop SF 41.HR. tyre is the high speed version of the Dunlop SP 41. The Standard SP 41 must not be used on 'E' Type cars unless the maximum speed is restricted to 125 mph (200 kph).

TYRES FOR WINTER USE

(when snow conditions make the use of special tyres necessary)

Dunlop Weathermaster 6.40 x 15

(For use only on rear wheels to replace Road Speed RS.5 tyres) 35 lb./sq. in. (2.46 kg./sq. cm.)

Maximum permitted speed 75 mph (120 kph)

Dunlop Weathermaster SP 44. 185 x 15

(For use only on rear wheels to replace SP 41.HR. tyres) 32 lb./sq. in. (2.25 kg./sq. cm.)

Maximum permitted speed 100 mph (160 kph).

Capacities

	Imperial	U.S.	Litres
Engine (refill including filter) ..	15 pints	18 pints	8.5
Gearbox ..	2½ ,,	3 ,,	1.42
Automatic transmission unit (2+2 only)	16 ,,	19 ,,	9
Rear axle	2¾ ,,	3¼ ,,	1.54
Cooling system (including heater)	32 ,,	38½ ,,	18.18
Petrol tank	14 galls.	16¾ galls.	63.64

Dimensions and Weights

Wheelbase (Open and fixed head coupe)	8′ 0″	(2.44 m.)
(2+2)	8′ 9″	(2.66 m.)
Track, Front	4′ 2″	(1.27 m.)
Track, Rear	4′ 2″	(1.27 m.)
Overall length (Open and fixed head coupe)	14′ 7$\frac{5}{16}$″	(4.45 m.)
(2+2)	15′ 4$\frac{7}{16}$″	(4.78 m.)
Overall width	5′ 5¼″	(1.66 m.)
Overall height (Fixed head coupe)	4′ 0⅛″	(1.22 m.)
(Open 2 seater)	3′ 10½″	(1.18 m.)
(2+2)	4′ 2⅛″	(1.27 m.)
Weight (dry) approximate (Fixed head coupe)	22½ cwts	(1123 kg.)
(Open 2 seater)	22 cwts	(1098 kg.)
(2+2 Standard transmission)	24½ cwts	(1245 kg.)
(2+2 Automatic transmission)	24¾ cwts	(1257 kg.)
Turning circle	37′ 0″	(11.27 m.)
(2+2)	41′ 0″	(12.19 m.)
Ground clearance	5½″	(140 mm.)

Lamp Bulbs

LAMP	LUCAS BULB NUMBER	VOLTS	WATTS	APPLICATION
Head	Sealed Beam Unit 410 411	12 12 12 12	75/45 50/40 45/40 45/40 (Yellow)	Home and RHD Export Middle East, S. America and U.S.A. Belgium, Holland, Sweden, Austria and Italy France
Side	989	12	6	
Front and Rear Flashing Indicators .. .. Reversing Light	382	12	21	
Rear/Brake..	380	12	21/6	
Number Plate Illumination	207	12	6	
Interior Lights	382 989	12 12	21 6	Open 2 Seater Fixed Head Coupé
Map Light	989	12	6	

Instrument Illumination :
  Headlamp warning light
  Ignition warning light
  Fuel level warning light
  Handbrake/Brake Fluid warning light ..
  Mixture control warning light .. .. ..
  Electrically heated backlight indicator light ..
  Traffic warning device indicator light ..
	987	12	2.2	

Switch indicator strip .. Flashing indicator warning light	281	12	2	
Automatic transmission selector quadrant ..	283	24	3	2 + 2 only

PERFORMANCE DATA

The following tables give the relationship between engine revolutions per minute and road speed in miles and kilometres per hour.

The safe maximum engine speed is 5,500 revolutions per minute.

Engines must not, under ANY CIRCUMSTANCES, be allowed to exceed this figure.

It is recommended that engine revolutions **in excess of 5,000 per minute** should not be exceeded for long periods. Therefore, if travelling at sustained high speed on motorways, the accelerator should be released occasionally to allow the car to overrun for a few seconds.

AXLE RATIO 3.31 : 1 (Open and Fixed Head Coupe)

ROAD SPEED		ENGINE REVOLUTIONS PER MINUTE			
K.p.h.	M.p.h.	1st Gear 8·87:1	2nd Gear 5·76:1	3rd Gear 4·20:1	Top Gear 3·31:1
16	10	1165	756	552	435
32	20	2330	1513	1104	870
48	30	3495	2269	1656	1305
64	40	4660	3026	2208	1738
80	50		3782	2758	2173
96	60		4539	3309	2608
112	70		5295	3861	3043
128	80			4412	3477
144	90			4964	3912
160	100				4347
176	110				4781
192	120				5216

Note: The figures in these tables are theoretical and actual figures may vary slightly from those quoted due to such factors as tyre wear, pressures etc.

PERFORMANCE DATA

The safe maximum engine speed is 5,500 revolutions per minute,
Engines must not, under ANY CIRCUMSTANCES, be allowed to exceed this figure.

It is recommended that engine revolutions **in excess of 5,000** per minute should not be exceeded for long periods. Therefore if travelling at sustained high speed on motorways, the accelerator should be released occasionally to allow the car to overrun for a few seconds.

AXLE RATIO 3.07 : 1 (Open and Fixed Head Coupe)

ROAD SPEED		ENGINE REVOLUTIONS PER MINUTE			
K.p.h.	M.p.h.	1st Gear 8·23:1	2nd Gear 5·34:1	3rd Gear 3·90:1	Top Gear 3·07:1
16	10	1081	701	512	401
32	20	2162	1403	1024	802
48	30	3243	2104	1536	1203
64	40	4324	2805	2049	1604
80	50	5405	3506	2561	2005
96	60		4207	3073	2407
112	70		4909	3585	2808
128	80			4097	3209
144	90			4609	3610
160	100			5122	4012
176	110				4412
192	120				4813
208	130				5214

Note: The figures in these tables are theoretical and actual figures may vary slightly from those quoted due to such factors as tyre wear, pressures etc.

The safe maximum engine speed is 5,500 revolutions per minute.

Engines must not, under ANY CIRCUMSTANCES, be allowed to exceed this figure.

It is recommended that engine revolutions **in excess of 5,000 per minute** should not be exceeded for long periods. Therefore if travelling at sustained high speed on motorways, the accelerator should be released occasionally to allow the car to overrun for a few seconds.

AXLE RATIO 3.54 : 1 (Open and Fixed Head Coupe)

ROAD SPEED		ENGINE REVOLUTIONS PER MINUTE			
K.p.h.	M.p.h.	1st Gear 9·49:1	2nd Gear 6·16:1	3rd Gear 4·50:1	Top Gear 3·54:1
16	10	1250	811	592	466
32	20	2500	1621	1185	932
48	30	3749	2432	1777	1398
64	40	4992	3240	2367	1862
80	50		4035	2947	2319
96	60		4829	3528	2775
112	70			4095	3221
128	80			4662	3667
144	90			5224	4110
160	100				4542
176	110				4963
192	120				5381

Note: The figures in these tables are theoretical and actual figures may vary slightly from those quoted due to such factors as tyre wear, pressures etc.

PERFORMANCE DATA

The safe maximum engine speed is 5,500 revolutions per minute.

Engines must not, under ANY CIRCUMSTANCES, be allowed to exceed this figure.

It is recommended that engine revolutions **in excess of 5,000 per minute** should not be exceeded for long periods. Therefore if travelling at sustained high speed on motorways, the accelerator should be released occasionally to allow the car to overrun for a few seconds.

AXLE RATIO 3.54 : 1 (2+2)

ROAD SPEED		ENGINE REVOLUTIONS PER MINUTE			
		1st Gear 10·76 : 1	2nd Gear 6·984 : 1	3rd Gear 4·701 : 1	Top Gear 3·54 : 1
K.p.h.	M.p.h.				
16	10	1413	917	617	465
32	20	2826	1834	1235	930
48	30	4239	2752	1852	1395
64	40	5652	3639	2470	1860
80	50		4586	3087	2325
96	60		5503	3704	2789
112	70			4322	3254
128	80			4939	3719
144	90			5557	4194
160	100				4649
176	110				5114
192	120				5579

Note : The figures in these tables are theoretical and actual figures may vary slightly from those quoted due to such factors as tyre wear, pressures etc.

The safe maximum engine speed is 5,500 revolutions per minute.

Engines must not, under ANY CIRCUMSTANCES, be allowed to exceed this figure.

It is recommended that engine revolutions **in excess of 5,000** per minute should not be exceeded for long periods. Therefore if travelling at sustained high speed on motorways, the accelerator should be released occasionally to allow the car to overrun for a few seconds.

AXLE RATIO 3.07 : 1 (2+2)

ROAD SPEED		ENGINE REVOLUTIONS PER MINUTE			
K.p.h.	M.p.h.	1st Gear 9·33 : 1	2nd Gear 6·057 : 1	3rd Gear 4·077 : 1	Top Gear 3.07 : 1
16	10	1225	795	535	403
32	20	2451	1591	1071	806
48	30	3675	2386	1606	1210
64	40	4901	3182	2142	1613
80	50		3977	2677	2016
96	60		4773	3212	2419
112	70		5568	3748	2822
128	80			4283	3226
144	90			4819	3629
160	100			5354	4032
176	110				4435
192	120				4838
208	130				5242

Note: The figures in these tables are theoretical and actual figures may vary slightly from those quoted due to such factors as tyre wear, pressures etc.

Automatic Transmission Data

2 + 2 only

Maximum ratio of torque convertor	2.00 : 1
1st Gear reduction	2.40 : 1
2nd Gear reduction	1.46 : 1
3rd Gear	1.00 : 1
Reverse gear reduction	2.00 : 1

Automatic Shift Speeds

185 × 15 S.P. Tyres   2.88 : 1 Final Drive Ratio

Selector Position	Throttle Position	Upshifts			Downshifts	
		1—2	2—3	3—2	3—1	2—1
MILES PER HOUR						
D1	Minimum	7—9	12—15	8—14	—	4—8
	Full	38—44	66—71	23—37	—	—
	Kickdown	52—56	81—89	73—81	20—24	20—24
D2	Minimum	—	12—15	8—14	—	—
	Full	—	66—71	23—37	—	—
	Kickdown	—	81—89	73—81	—	—
L	Zero	—	—	Any	—	12—20
KILOMETRES PER HOUR						
D1	Minimum	11—14	19—24	13—23	—	6—13
	Full	39—70	106—114	37—60	—	—
	Kickdown	83—90	130—143	118—130	32—39	32—39
D2	Minimum	—	19—24	13—23	—	—
	Full	—	106—114	37—60	—	—
	Kickdown	—	130—143	118—130	—	—
L	Zero	—	—	Any	—	19—32

Automatic Shift Speeds

185 × 15 S.P. Tyres   3.31 : 1 Final Drive Ratio

Selector Position	Throttle Position	Upshifts			Downshifts	
		1—2	2—3	3—2	3—1	2—1
		MILES PER HOUR				
DI	Minimum	6—8	11—13	7—13	—	3—7
	Full	33—40	58—62	19—33	—	—
	Kickdown	45—49	70—78	63—71	17—21	17—21
D2	Minimum	—	11—13	7—13	—	—
	Full	—	58—62	19—33	—	—
	Kickdown	—	70—78	63—71	—	—
L	Zero	—	—	Any	—	10—18
		KILOMETRES PER HOUR				
D1	Minimum	9—13	18—21	11—21	—	5—11
	Full	53—64	93—100	31—53	—	—
	Kickdown	73—80	113—126	101—114	28—34	28—34
D2	Minimum	—	18—21	11—21	—	—
	Full	—	93—100	31—53	—	—
	Kickdown	—	113—126	101—114	—	—
L	Zero	—	—	Any	—	16—29

CAUTION

The brakes of this car are assisted in operation by a Vacuum Servo which will only operate when the engine is running.

Increased pressure on the brake pedal is required to operate the brakes when the Servo is not in action.

Do not coast the car in neutral with the engine switched off.

IMPORTANT

BRAKES

To obtain satisfactory braking from high speeds your car is fitted with brake friction pads which are manufactured of a hard material having a relatively low coefficient of friction.

To obtain fully satisfactory results it is important that careful attention is paid to the following points during the first 1,000 miles running of your car.

1. Other than in the case of emergency, avoid heavy braking. (Heavy braking or rough usage of the brakes before the friction pads are fully bedded can result in damage being caused to the friction pads and brake discs.)

2. Frequent light application of the brakes is desirable to obtain full bedding of the brake friction pads before the normal running-in period is completed and the car operated at high speeds, when maximum brake efficiency will be required.

OPERATING INSTRUCTIONS

INSTRUMENTS

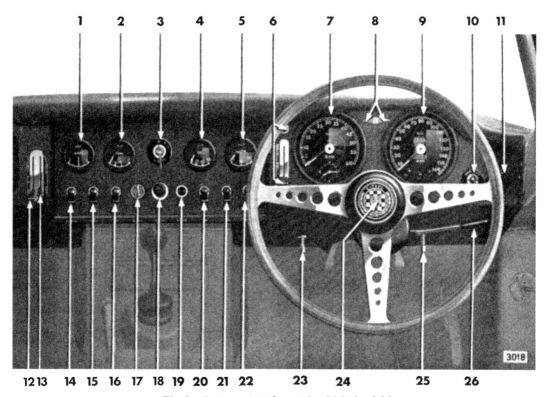

Fig. 2.   Instruments and controls—Right-hand drive

1. *Ammeter.*
2. *Fuel contents gauge.*
3. *Lighting switch.*
4. *Oil pressure gauge.*
5. *Water temperature gauge.*
6. *Mixture control and warning light.*
7. *Revolution counter.*
8. *Flashing direction indicator warning lights.*
9. *Speedometer.*
10. *Brake fluid warning light.*
11. *Headlamp dipper switch.*
12. *Heater—Air control.*
13. *Heater—Temperature control.*
14. *Interior light switch*
15. *Panel light switch.*
16. *Heater fan switch.*
17. *Ignition switch.*
18. *Cigar Lighter.*
19. *Starter switch.*
20. *Map light switch.*
21. *Windscreen wiper switch.*
22. *Windscreen washer switch.*
23. *Clock adjuster.*
24. *Horn button.*
25. *Speedometer trip control.*
26. *Flashing direction indicator and headlamp flashing switch.*

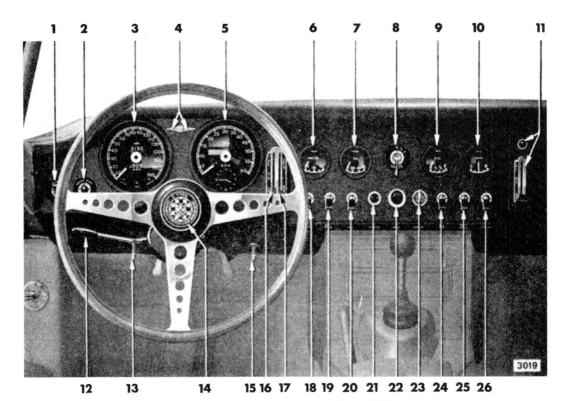

Fig. 3.   Instruments and controls—Left-hand drive

1. Headlamp dipper switch.
2. Brake fluid warning light.
3. Speedometer.
4. Flashing direction indicator warning lights.
5. Revolution counter.
6. Water temperature gauge.
7. Oil pressure gauge.
8. Lighting switch.
9. Fuel contents gauge.
10. Ammeter.
11. Mixture control and warning light.
12. Flashing direction indicator and headlamp flashing switch.
13. Speedometer trip control.

14. Horn button.
15. Clock adjuster.
16. Heater—air control.
17. Heater—temperature control.
18. Windscreen washer switch.
19. Windscreen wiper switch.
20. Map light switch.
21. Starter switch.
22. Cigar lighter.
23. Ignition switch.
24. Heater fan switch.
25. Panel light switch.
26. Interior light switch.

Ammeter

Records the flow of current into or out of the battery. Since compensated voltage control is incorporated, the flow of current is adjusted to the state of charge of the battery; thus when the battery is fully charged the alternator provides only a small output and little charge is registered on the ammeter, whereas when the battery is low a continuous high charge is shown.

Oil Pressure Gauge

The electrically operated pressure gauge records the oil pressure being delivered by the oil pump to the engine; it does not record the quantity of oil in the sump. The minimum pressure at 3,000 r.p.m. when hot should not be less than 40 lb. per square inch.

Note : After switching on, a period of approximately 20 seconds will elapse before the correct reading is obtained.

Water Temperature Gauge

The electrically operated water temperature gauge records the temperature of the coolant by means of a bulb screwed into the inlet manifold water jacket.

Fuel Level Gauge

Records the quantity of fuel in the supply tank. Readings will only be obtained when the ignition is switched " on ".

Note : After switching on, a period of approximately 20 seconds will elapse before the correct reading is obtained.

Electric Clock

The clock is built in the revolution counter instrument and is powered by the battery. The clock hands may be adjusted by pushing up the winder and rotating. Starting is accomplished in the same manner.

Revolution Counter

Records the speed of the engine in revolutions per minute.

Speedometer

Records the vehicle speed in miles per hour, total mileage and trip mileage (kilometres on certain export models). The trip figures can be set to zero by pushing the winder upwards and rotating.

Headlamp Warning Light

A warning light marked " Headlamps " situated in the speedometer, lights up when the headlamps are in full beam position and is automatically extinguished when the lamps are in the dipped beam position.

Ignition Warning Light

A red warning light (marked " Ignition ") situated in the speedometer lights up when the ignition is switched " on " and the engine is not running, or when the engine is running at a speed insufficient to charge the battery. The latter condition is not harmful, but always switch "off" when the engine is not running.

Fuel Level Warning Light

An amber warning light (marked " Fuel ") situated in the speedometer lights up intermittently when the fuel level in the tank becomes low. When the fuel is almost exhausted the warning light operates continuously.

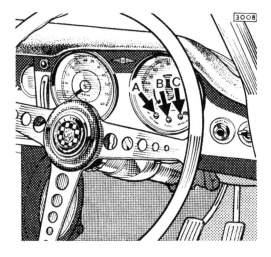

Fig. 4. *Warning lights.*

A. *Ignition.*　　B. *Fuel.*　　C. *Headlamps.*

Flashing Indicator Warning Lights

The warning lights are in the form of green arrows located on the facia panel situated behind the steering wheel.

When the flasher indicators are in operation one of the arrows lights up on the side selected.

Fig. 5. *Brake Fluid Handbrake Warning light.*

Brake Fluid Level and Handbrake Warning Light

A warning light (marked " Brake Fluid—Handbrake ") situated on the facia behind the steering wheel, serves to indicate if the level in either of the two brake fluid reservoirs has become low, provided the ignition is " on ". As the warning light is also illuminated when the handbrake is applied, the handbrake must be fully released before it is assumed that fluid level is low. If with the ignition " on " and the handbrake fully released the warning light is illuminated the brake fluid must be " topped up " and the reason for the loss investigated and corrected immediately. IT IS ESSENTIAL that the correct specification of brake fluid be used when topping up.

As the warning light is illuminated when the handbrake is applied and the ignition is " on " a two fold purpose is served. Firstly, to avoid the possibility of driving away with the handbrake applied. Secondly, as a check that the warning light bulb has not " blown "; if on first starting up the car with the handbrake fully applied, the warning light does not become illuminated the bulb should be changed immediately.

CONTROLS AND ACCESSORIES

Accelerator Pedal

Controls the speed of the engine.

Brake Pedal

Operates the vacuum servo assisted disc brakes on all four wheels.

Clutch Pedal

On standard transmission cars connects and disconnects the engine and the transmission. Never drive with the foot resting on the pedal and do not keep the pedal depressed for long periods in traffic. Never coast the car with a gear engaged and clutch depressed.

Headlamp Dipper

Situated on the facia panel behind the steering wheel. The switch is of the " flick-over " type, and if the headlamps are on main beam, moving the lever will switch the dipped beam on, and main beam off. They will remain so until the switch lever is reversed.

Gear Lever (Standard Transmission Cars)

Centrally situated and with the gear positions indicated on the control knob. To engage reverse gear first press the gear lever against the spring pressure before pulling the lever rearward. Always engage neutral and release the clutch when the car is at rest.

Automatic Transmission Selector Lever (2+2)

For full instructions on the operation of the automatic transmission, see page 19.

Handbrake Lever

Positioned centrally between seats. The handbrake operates mechanically on the rear wheels only and is provided for parking, driving away on a hill and when at a standstill in traffic. To apply the brake, pull the lever upward and the trigger will automatically engage with the ratchet. The handbrake

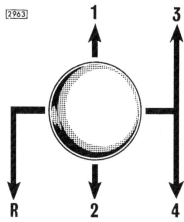

Fig. 6. *Gear positions.*

is released by pressing in the knob, and pushing the lever downward.

Seat Adjustment

Both front seats are adjustable for reach. Push the lock bar, situated beside the inside runner, towards the inside of the car and slide into the required position. Release the lock bar and slide until the mechanism engages with a click.

The rake of the seat back is adjustable by means of the arrangement illustrated in Fig. 8.

Long-legged drivers who require the maximum amount of leg room, combined with the maximum rake of the seat back, may find it advantageous to locate the seat one notch forward from the rearmost position with the rake adjustment in the lowest position (B Figure 8).

Alternatively, if a more upright seat position is desired, the best results may be obtained by setting the rake adjuster in the highest position (A Figure 8) with the seat located in the rearmost position.

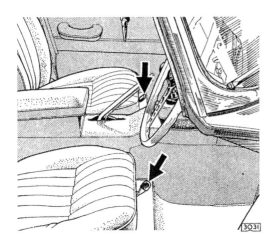

Fig. 7.   *Seat adjustment (fore and aft).*

Fig. 9.   *Steering wheel adjustment.*

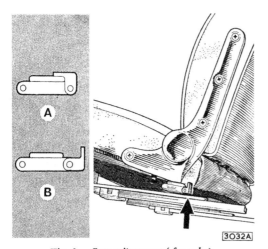

Fig. 8.   *Seat adjustment (for rake).*

Steering Wheel Adjustment

Rotate the knurled ring at the base of the steering wheel hub in an anti-clockwise direction when the steering wheel may be slid into the desired position.   Turn the knurled ring clockwise to lock the steering wheel.

Door Locks (Open and Fixed Head Coupe)

The doors may be opened from the outside by pressing the button incorporated in the door handle.   The doors are opened from the inside by pulling the interior handles rearward.

Both doors can be locked from the inside by pushing the interior handles forward and allowing them to return to their original position ; this feature only applies if the doors are fully closed before operating the interior handles.   Both doors can be locked from the outside by means of the ignition key ; the locks are incorporated in the push buttons of the door handles.

To lock the right-hand door insert the key in the lock, rotate anti-clockwise as far as possible and allow the lock to return to its original position—the door is now locked.

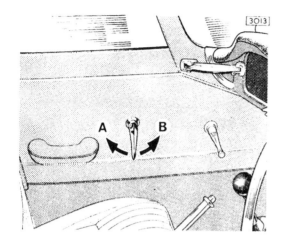

Fig. 10. *Door locks (internal).*
A — to open   B — to lock

To unlock the right-hand door turn key clockwise as far as possible and allow the lock to return to its original position.

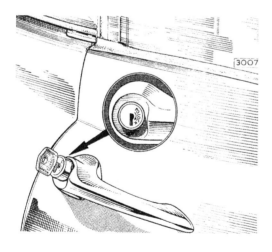

Fig. 11. *Door locks (external Open and Fixed Head Coupe only).*

To lock the left-hand door rotate key clockwise ; to unlock, rotate key anti-clockwise.

KEYLESS LOCKING is obtainable by first pushing the interior door handle fully forward and allowing it to return to its original position. If the door is now closed from the outside with the push button of the handle **fully depressed** the door will become locked.

Warning.—If the doors are to be locked by this method the ignition key should be removed beforehand (or the spare key kept on the driver's person) as the only means of unlocking the doors is with this key.

Door Locks (2 + 2)

The separate individual door locks are incorporated in the door panels, keyless locking not being obtainable.

Horn

Depress the circular button in the centre of the steering wheel to operate the horns.

Note.— The horns will not operate if ignition is off.

Ignition Switch

Inserting the key provided in the switch and turning clockwise will switch on the ignition.

Never leave the ignition on when the engine has stopped, a reminder of such circumstances is provided by the ignition warning light situated in the speedometer.

Interior Light Switch

Lift the switch lever (marked " Interior") to illuminate the car interior.

Lighting Switch

From " Off " can be rotated into two positions, giving in the first location side and tail, and in the second location head, side and tail.

Panel Light Switch

Lift the switch lever (marked " Panel ") to enable the instruments to be read at night and to provide illumination of the switch markings. The switch has two positions " Dim " and " Bright " to suit the driver's requirements. The panel lights will only operate when the side lights are switched on.

Starter Switch

Press the button (marked " Starter ") with the ignition switched on, to start the engine. Release the switch immediately the engine fires and never operate the starter when the engine is running.

Map Light

Lift the switch lever (marked " Map ") to illuminate the lamp situated above the instrument panel. To provide ease of entry into the car at night the map light is switched on when either one of the doors is opened, and is extinguished when the door is closed.

Flashing Direction Indicator

The " flashers " are operated by a lever behind the steering wheel. To operate the flashing direction indicators on the right-hand side of the car, move the lever clockwise ; to operate the left-hand side indicators move the lever anti-clockwise. While the flashing indicators are in operation, one of the warning lights on the facia panel behind the steering wheel will flash on the side selected.

Fig. 12. *Flashing direction indicator control.*

Headlamp Flasher

To " flash " the headlamps as a warning signal, lift and release the flashing indicator lever in quick succession. The headlamps can be " flashed " when the lights are " off " or when they are in the dipped beam position ; they will not " flash " in the main beam position.

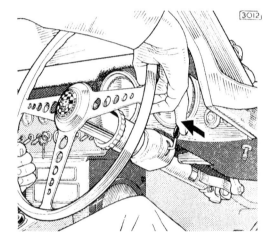

Fig. 13. *Method of " flashing " the headlamps.*

Braking Lights

Twin combined tail and brake lights automatically function when the footbrake is applied.

Luggage Compartment Illumination

The luggage compartment is illuminated by the interior light when this lamp is switched on.

Mixture Control Warning Light

A red warning light situated above the mixture control on the facia panel behind the steering wheel serves to indicate if the mixture is in operation. This warning light is illuminated immediately the control lever is moved from " off " position.

To change the bulb, accessible behind the facia panel, pull bulb holder away from " clip in " attachment, and unscrew bulb by turning anti-clockwise. For full instructions on the use of the mixture control see " Starting and Driving " page 37.

Cigar Lighter

To operate, press holder (marked " Cigar ") into the socket and remove the hand. On reaching the required temperature, the holder will return to the extended position. Do not hold the lighter in the " pressed-in " position.

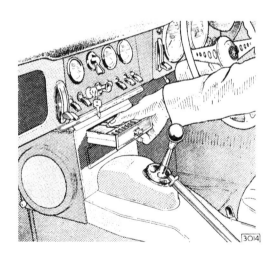

Fig. 14. *Removal of the ash tray.*

29

Windscreen Wipers

The wipers are controlled by a three position switch (marked " Wiper "). Lift the switch to the second position (Slow) which is recommended for all normal adverse weather conditions and snow.

For conditions of very heavy rain and for fast driving in rain lift the switch to the third position (Fast). This position should not be used in heavy snow or with a drying windscreen, that is, when the load on motor is in excess of normal ; the motor incorporates a protective cut-out switch which under conditions of excessive load cuts off the current supply until normal conditions are restored.

When the switch is placed in the " Off " position the wipers will automatically return to a position along the lower edge of the screen.

Note: The wiper blades are manufactured with special anti-smear properties. Renew only with genuine Jaguar parts.

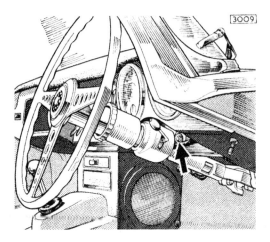

Fig. 15. *Steering column adjustment for rake.*

Windscreen Washer

For full instructions on the use of Windscreen Washing Equipment see page 48.

Heating and Ventilating Equipment

For full instructions on the use of the Heating and Ventilating Equipment see page 45.

Steering Column—Adjustment for Rake

The steering column can be adjusted for rake. To adjust, release nut and bolt at the top of the column located behind the instrument panel, and adjust to suit requirements. Re-tighten nut fully after adjustment.

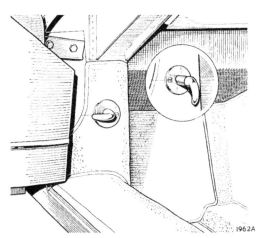

Fig. 16. *Showing the bonnet lock lever in the locked position. The inset shows the lever in the unlocked position.*

Bonnet Lock

To open the bonnet turn the two small levers located on the right and left-hand door hinge posts anti-clockwise and pull to full extent. This will release the bonnet which will now be retained by the safety catch.

Insert the fingers under the rear edge of the bonnet and press in the safety catch.

To close the bonnet, ensure that the levers are pulled out to their full extent, push down to the safety catch position, push in the two levers and turn clockwise.

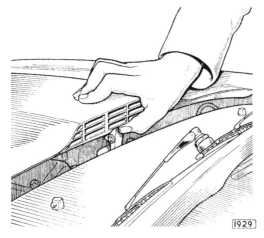

Fig. 17. *Bonnet safety catch.*

Radiator Fan

The radiator fan is electrically driven, the cutting in speed being controlled automatically by means of a thermostatic switch incorporated in the engine cooling system.

The fan will not operate with the ignition switched OFF. When the coolant reaches a temperature of approximately 80°C. the thermostatic switch closes and starts the fan motor. The fan motor will continue to run until the temperature has fallen below approximately 72°C.

No routine maintenance is necessary. In the event of a failure :

1. Check fan motor earth is clean and tighten if loose.

2. Check fuse No. 6 (see page 95) and replace if blown.

If after fitting a replacement fuse the fan still does not work, this indicates a fault in one of the components and the car should therefore be taken to the nearest Jaguar dealer for examination.

Driving Mirror Adjustment (Open 2-seater)

This is of the dipping type. Move lever, situated under mirror, forward for night driving to avoid being dazzled by the lights of a following car.

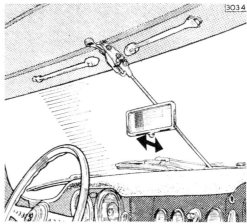

Fig. 18. *Interior driving mirror dipping operation (open 2-seater).*

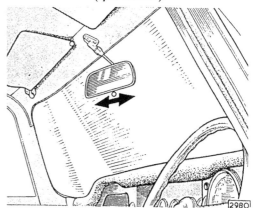

Fig. 19. *Interior driving mirror dipping operation (fixed head coupe and 2 + 2).*

Driving Mirror Adjustment
(Fixed Head Coupe and 2 + 2)

This is of the dipping type. Move lever situated under the mirror, to the left for night driving to avoid being dazzled by the lights of a following car.

Fuel Tank Filler

The fuel tank filler is situated in a recess in the left-hand rear wing and is provided with a hinged cover.

Tools

The tools are contained in a tool roll placed in the spare wheel compartment.

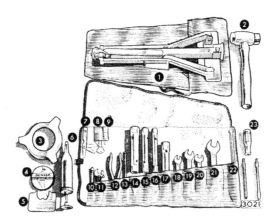

Fig. 20.   *The Tool Kit.*

1. Jack.	13. Tommy bar (short).
2. Hammer (Copper and Rawhide).	14. Box Spanner (Sparking plugs and cylinder head nuts).
3. Hub cap removal tool.	
4. Bleeder tube.	15. Box spanner ($\frac{9}{16}'' \times \frac{5}{8}''$ S.A.E.)
5. Valve timing gauge.	16. Box spanner ($\frac{7}{16}'' \times \frac{1}{2}''$ S.A.E.)
6. Grease gun.	17. Box spanner ($\frac{3}{4}'' \times \frac{7}{8}''$ S.A.E.)
7. Feeler gauge.	18. Open ended spanner ($\frac{11}{32}'' \times \frac{3}{8}''$ A.F.)
8. Screwdriver for contact breaker points.	19. Open ended spanner ($\frac{9}{16}'' \times \frac{5}{8}''$ A.F.)
9. Tyre valve extractor.	20. Open ended spanner ($\frac{1}{2}'' \times \frac{7}{16}''$ A.F.)
10. Tyre pressure gauge.	21. Open ended spanner ($\frac{3}{4}'' \times \frac{7}{8}''$ A.F.)
11. Adjustable spanner.	22. Tommy bar (long).
12. Pliers.	23. Combination screwdriver.

Spare Wheel and Jacking Equipment

The spare wheel is housed in a compartment under the luggage boot floor, and is accessible after removal of the square lid.

The copper hammer and jack are retained in clips in the luggage boot.

Fig. 21. *Spare wheel housing (Open 2-seater).*

Fig. 22. *Spare wheel housing (Fixed head coupe).*

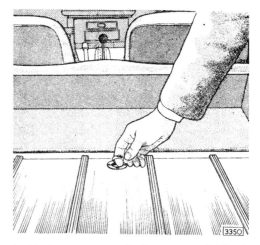

Fig. 23. *Removing spare wheel compartment lid (2 + 2).*

Luggage Compartment (Open 2-seater)

The luggage compartment is unlocked by turning the key in the direction of arrow "A" (Fig. 24) and pulling the lock barrel outwards in the direction of arrow "B".

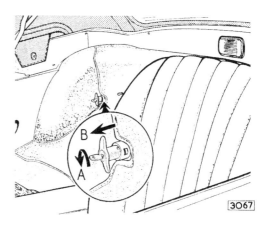

Fig. 24. *Luggage compartment lock control (Open 2-seater).*

Luggage Compartment Fixed (Head Coupe and 2+2)

The luggage compartment is unlocked by lifting the recessed chromium plated lever situated in the body trim panel beside the right-hand seat. To operate, insert finger and lift out the lever to the full extent. The lid will now be retained in position by the safety catch.

Insert the fingers under the right-hand edge of the lid and press in the safety catch.

The lid is retained in the open position by means of a self-locking stay.

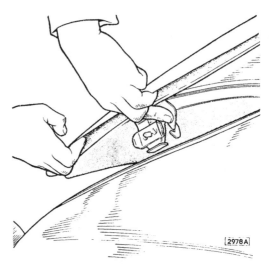

Fig. 26. *Luggage compartment lid safety catch (Fixed head coupe and 2 + 2).*

Fig. 25. *Luggage compartment lock control (Fixed Head coupe.)*

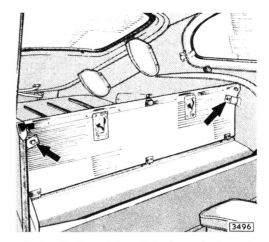

Fig. 27. *Back panel fixing bolts (Fixed head coupe).*

SEAT BELTS

Anchorage points for seat belts are incorporated in the construction of the car. If it is required to fit seat belts, contact your usual Jaguar dealer.

Seat Back Panel (Fixed Head Coupe)

The back panel behind the seat normally serves as a partition behind the driving and luggage compartment. The panel can be lowered to give an increased boot floor area if required for extra storage.

To lower release the two side fixing bolts and drop panel forward. Stop arms should be raised to prevent luggage contacting back of seats. Return panel to vertical position when extra boot space is not required.

Rear Seat Squabs (2+2)

The rear seat squab normally serves as a partition between the driving and luggage compartments.

The top section of the squab can be hinged forward to give an increased luggage compartment floor area if required for extra stowage.

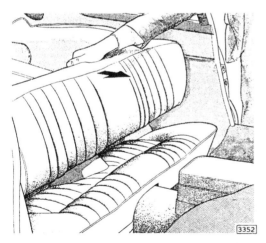

Fig. 28. *Moving the rear seat squab forward.*

Traffic Hazard Warning Device (U.S.A. Market Only)

The traffic hazard warning system operates in conjunction with the four flashing turn indicator lamps fitted to the car and the operation of a toggle switch on a sub-panel will cause these four lamps to flash simultaneously.

A red warning lamp is incorporated in the circuit to indicate that the hazard warning system is in operation.

Fig. 29. *The traffic hazard warning device control panel.*

Electrically Heated Backlight (Optional Extra)

An electrically heated backlight to provide demisting and defrosting of the rear window is available as an optional extra.

A heating element, consisting of a fine wire mesh between the laminations of glass, is connected to the wiring harness and functions only when the ignition and heater switches are in the "ON" position.

An amber warning lamp, situated on the facia panel, lights up when the backlight heater is switched on. A resistance in the circuit through the side and headlamp switch automatically dims the warning lamp for night driving.

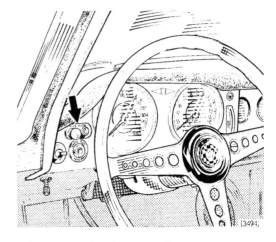

Fig. 30. *Backlight heater switch and warning lamp.*

STARTING AND DRIVING

Prior to Starting

Ensure that the coolant level in the radiator and the oil level in the sump are correct. Check for sufficient petrol in the tank.

Starting from Cold

A manual mixture control is provided located in facia panel behind steering wheel. This control has six positions; the "fully rich" position being at the top of the slide marked "COLD". Moving the lever progressively downwards weakens the mixture strength. The two positions from "HOT" give a fast idle condition; the last position "RUN" being off.

A red warning light is incorporated in the control which lights up immediately the lever is moved from "RUN" position.

When starting from cold the mixture control should be moved to the fully rich "COLD" position. Switch on the ignition and press the starter button, but do not touch the accelerator. Release the starter button as soon as the engine fires—this is important. If for any reason the engine does not start **do not operate the starter button again until both the engine and starter motor have come to rest.**

As soon as the engine speed increases slide the control progressively to the intermediate "HOT" position.

Drive off at a moderate speed progressively sliding the mixture control to the "RUN" position until the knob is at the bottom of the slide and the red warning light is extinguished.

Always return the control to "RUN" position as soon as possible. Unnecessary use of the mixture control will result in reduced engine life.

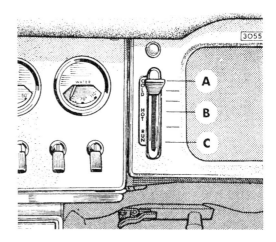

Fig. 31. *Mixture control positions.*
A—Cold   B—Hot   C—Run

Starting in Moderate Temperature

In warm weather or if the engine is not absolutely cold, it is usually possible to start the engine with the mixture control in one of the intermediate "HOT" positions. Do not touch the accelerator pedal.

OPERATING INSTRUCTIONS

Starting When Hot

Do not use the mixture control. If the engine does not start immediately slightly depress the accelerator pedal when making the next attempt.

Warming up

Do not operate the engine at a fast speed when first started but allow time for the engine to warm up and the oil to circulate. A thermostat is incorporated in the cooling system to assist rapid warming up. In very cold weather run the engine at 1,500 r.p.m. with the car stationary until a rise in temperature is indicated on the temperature gauge.

Driving

(a) Careful adherence to the " Running-in " Instructions given will be amply repaid by obtaining the best performance and utmost satisfaction from the car.

(b) The habit should be formed of reading the oil pressure gauge, water temperature gauge and ammeter occasionally as a check on the correct functioning of the car. Should an abnormal reading be obtained an investigation should be made immediately.

(c) On standard transmission cars always start from rest in first gear; to start in a higher gear will cause excessive clutch slip and premature wear. Never drive with a foot resting on the clutch pedal and do not keep the clutch depressed for long periods in traffic.

(d) The synchromesh gearbox provides a synchronized change in all forward gears.

When changing down a smoother gear change will be obtained if the accelerator is left depressed to provide the higher engine speed suitable to the lower gear. Always fully depress the clutch pedal when changing gear.

(e) Gear changing may be slightly stiff on a new car but this will disappear as the gearbox becomes " run-in ".

(f) Always apply the footbrake progressively ; fierce and sudden application is bad for the car and tyres. The handbrake is for use when parking the car, when driving away on a hill and when at a standstill in traffic.

" Running-in " Instructions

Only if the following important recommendations are observed will the high performance and continued good running of which the Jaguar is capable be obtained.

During the " running-in " period do not allow the engine to exceed the following speeds and particularly do not allow the engine to labour on hills ; it is preferable to select a lower gear and use a higher speed rather than allow the engine to labour at low speed :—

First 1,000 miles (1,600 km.)	2,500 r.p.m.
From 1,000—2,000 miles (1,600—3,200 km.) ..	3,000 r.p.m.

Have the engine sump drained and refilled and the oil filter and seal renewed as recommended at the free service, that is, after the first 1,000 miles (1,600 km.).

AUTOMATIC TRANSMISSION (2 + 2)

Operation

The automatic transmission incorporates an hydraulic torque converter in place of the flywheel and clutch. This convertor is coupled to an hydraulically operated planetary gearbox which provides three forward speeds and a reverse.

Operation of the automatic transmission is controlled by the driver through the selector lever mounted centrally in the console.

The quadrant markings, from front to rear, are P, R, N, D2, D1, L.

The selector lever can be moved freely between N and D2. To move the lever between D2 and D1, D1 and L, or to the P or R positions, the control lever must be pressed to the right against the spring pressure.

Warning

Neither P nor R should be engaged whilst the car is in motion.

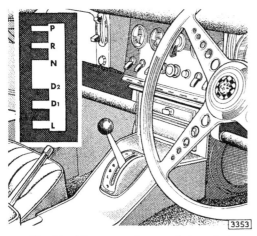

Fig. 32. *The automatic transmission selector.*

P (Park)

In the Park position the gearbox is mechanically locked by means of the parking pawl which engages with external teeth formed on the ring gear integral with the driven shaft.

Park should not be selected when the car is in motion.

Use of the Park position is recommended whenever the car is parked with or without the engine running.

R (Reverse)

The "R" position provides reverse ratio. Do not select Reverse when the car is moving forward.

N (Neutral)

All clutches are disengaged and there is no drive beyond the torque converter. The handbrake must be applied whenever Neutral is selected and the car is at rest.

D2 (Drive range, 2nd gear start)

In the Drive 2 position, the car starts from rest in second gear and operates automatically between second and third gears.

At, or below, a preset maximum vehicle speed, downshifts from 3rd to 2nd may be effected by depressing the accelerator fully. ("Kickdown" position).

First gear is not obtainable in this position but D2 is suitable for normal driving where maximum acceleration is not required.

In this position, the car will not roll back on hills as long as the engine is running.

D1 (Drive range, 1st gear start)

When in the D1 position, the car starts from rest in first gear and operates automatically through all three forward ratios. Upshifts and downshifts occur in accordance with car speed and throttle position.

At, or below, preset maximum road speeds downshifts may be effected from 3rd to 2nd, from 2nd to 1st, or, directly, from 3rd to 1st. This is accomplished by depressing the accelerator fully. ("Kickdown" position).

L (Lockup)

Lockup position provides overriding control for either first or second gear with engine braking in either ratio.

When starting from rest in the lockup position the transmission starts in 1st gear and remains in that gear regardless of road speed or throttle position. Maximum engine braking is available in this gear.

In either D1 or D2 with the transmission in 3rd gear, the selection of L will cause an immediate downshift to second gear. This will provide moderate engine braking when the throttle is closed.

If the road speed is reduced to approximately 16 m.p.h. (25 k.p.h.) the transmission will downshift automatically from second to first and provide maximum engine braking.

Once first gear is attained, no upshift will be possible until the selector lever is removed from the L position.

Starting

A starter inhibitor switch ensures that the starter will operate only when the selector is in either the P or N position.

Engine Braking

When engine braking is required whilst descending steep hills apply the footbrake to reduce speed to approximately 60 m.p.h. (96 k.p.h.) or below.

Move the selector lever to the L position to obtain an immediate downshift to second gear.

If the road speed is below 16 m.p.h. (25 k.p.h.) when L is selected the downshift will be directly from 3rd to 1st gear.

Rocking the Car

In order to extricate a car from mud, sand or snow, employ a constant slight throttle opening and rock the car backwards and forwards by alternately selecting the R and D2 positions.

Stopping

To bring the car to rest, release the accelerator and apply the brakes.

The selector lever may be left in L, D2, or D1 unless the car is to be parked.

Parking

When the car is stationary select the P (Park) position.

Push Starting

It is possible to effect an engine start by pushing the car.

To do this, select N and switch the ignition ON.

Depress accelerator pedal approximately $\frac{1}{3}$ and when the car reaches approximately 20 m.p.h. (32 k.p.h.) select D2 or L. Do NOT tow the car to start the engine—it may overtake the towing vehicle.

Towing

The car may be towed with a dead engine in an emergency. Before towing ensure that the transmission fluid is at the correct level. Towing should be done with the transmission selector in the N position and speed should not exceed 30 m.p.h. (48 k.p.h.).

If the car is being towed because of transmission damage, the propeller shaft should be removed or towing should be done by lifting the rear wheels from the ground. Failure to do this may result in further extensive transmission damage.

Warning

Do NOT select "P" or "R" whilst the car is in motion.

WHEEL CHANGING

Whenever possible the wheel changing should be carried out with the car standing on level ground, and in all cases with the hand-brake fully applied.

Unlock the luggage compartment as detailed previously.

The spare wheel is housed in a compartment underneath the luggage boot floor; the wheel changing equipment is retained in clips.

Remove the copper and hide mallet from the tool kit. Using the mallet, slacken but do not remove the hub caps; the hub caps are marked Right (off) side or Left (near) side, and the direction of rotation to remove, that is, clockwise for the right-hand side and anti-clockwise for the left-hand side.

The jacking sockets on open and fixed head coupé cars will be found centrally located on either side of the car.

On 2+2 cars four jacking pegs (two per side) are provided for raising the car.

The lifting pad of the jack is forked (inset, Fig. 34) and care must be taken to ensure that the fork is *fully located* on the peg

Fig. 34. Jacking the 2 + 2 at rear.

Fig. 33. *The jack in position for raising the right-hand side of car. (Fixed head coupe).*

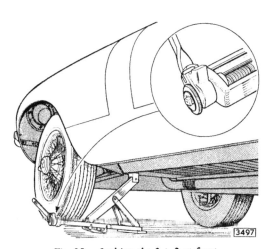

Fig. 35. Jacking the 2 + 2 at front.

before raising the car. The position of the lever (inset, Fig. 35) controls the operation of the jack screw for raising or lowering the car.

Fig. 36. *Hub cap—right-hand side.*

Place jack under car to locate in the socket (or peg) and raise car until wheels are clear of ground. Remove hub cap and withdraw wheel. Mount the spare wheel on the splined hub. Refit the hub cap and tighten as much as possible by rotating cap in the required direction, that is

Fig. 37. *Hub cap—left-hand side.*

anti-clockwise for the right-hand side and clockwise for the left-hand side.

Lower the jack and finally tighten the hub fully with the copper and hide mallet.

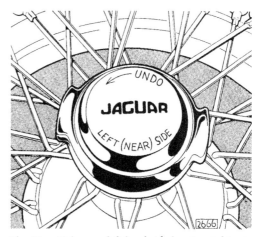

Fig. 38. *Hub cap—left hand-side (continental type).*

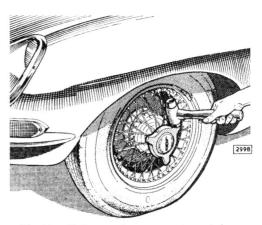

Fig. 39. *Tightening the continental type hub cap with the removal tool.*

FROST PRECAUTIONS

Anti-freeze—Important

During the winter months it is strongly recommended that an anti-freeze compound with an **inhibited Ethylene Glycol base** be used in the proportions laid down by the anti-freeze manufacturers.

It should be remembered that if anti-freeze is not used or is not of sufficient strength it is possible owing to the action of thermostat for the radiator to " freeze-up " whilst the car is being driven even though the water in the radiator was not frozen when the engine was started.

Before adding anti-freeze solution the cooling system should be cleaned by flushing. To do this, open the radiator block and cylinder block drain taps and insert a water hose into the radiator filler neck. Allow the water to flow through the system, with the engine running at 1,000 r.p.m. to cause circulation, until the water runs clear. The cylinder head gasket must be in good condition and the cylinder head nuts pulled down correctly, since if the solution leaks into the crankcase a mixture will be formed with the engine oil which is likely to cause blockage of the oil-ways with consequent damage to working parts. Check tightness of all water hose connections, water pump and manifold joints. To ensure satisfactory mixing, measure the recommended proportion of water and anti-freeze solution in a separate container and fill the system from this container, rather than add the solution direct to the cooling system. Check the radiator water level after running the engine and top up if necessary. Topping up must be carried out using anti-freeze solution or the degree of protection may be lost. Topping up with water will dilute the mixture possibly to an extent where damage by frost will occur.

Engine Heater

Provision is made on the right-hand side of the cylinder block for the fitment of an American standard engine heater element No. 7, manufactured by " James B. Carter Ltd., Electrical Heating and Manufacturing Division, Winnipeg, Manitoba, Canada " or " George Bray & Co. Ltd., Leicester Place, Blackman Lane, Leeds 2, England ".

Warning

The fitting of an engine heater does not obviate the use of 'anti-freeze' during the winter months.

CAR HEATING AND VENTILATING EQUIPMENT

Car Heating and Ventilating System

The car heating and ventilating equipment consists of a heating element and an electrically driven fan mounted on the engine side of the bulkhead. Air from the heater unit is conducted :

(a) To a built in duct situated behind the instrument panel.

(b) To vents at the bottom of the windscreen to provide demisting and defrosting.

The amount of fresh air can be controlled at the will of driver and is introduced into the system by operating the " Air " control lever and switching on the fan.

Air Control

The air control (A, Figs. 40 and 41), (marked " OFF-AIR-ON ") controls the amount of fresh air passing through the heater element ; when this control is placed in the " OFF " position the supply of air is completely cut off.

Placed in the " ON " position the maximum of air passes through the heater element. By placing the control in intermediate positions varying amounts of air may be obtained.

Temperature Control

The temperature control (B, Figs. 40 and 41), (marked " HOT—COLD ") situated on the facia panel operates a valve which controls the amount of hot water passing through the heater element ; when this control is placed in the " COLD " position the

supply of hot water to the element is completely cut off so that cold air only can be admitted for ventilating the car in hot weather.

Placed in the " HOT " position the maximum amount of hot water passes through the heater element. By placing the control in intermediate positions varying degrees of heat may be obtained.

Air Distribution (Open and Fixed Head Coupe)

The proportion of air directed to the windscreen or the interior of the car can be controlled by the position of the two doors situated under the duct behind the instrument panel.

With the heater doors fully closed the maximum amount of air will be directed to the windscreen for rapid demisting and defrosting.

With the heater doors fully open, air will be directed into the car interior and to a lesser degree to the windscreen.

Air Distribution (2+2)

The demisting outlets operate when the system is working. To obtain maximum air at the windscreen, the outlets under the duct behind the instrument panel should be fully closed.

These two outlets are fitted with finger operated direction controls on the facia panel. Fully rotating the right-hand knob clockwise and the left-hand knob anti-clockwise will cut off supply of air to the interior completely. Reverse rotation of the knobs will progressively re-direct the airflow from the feet to the body.

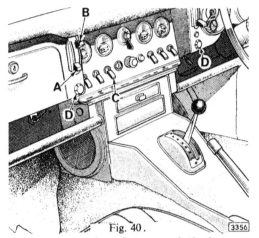

Fig. 40.

Heating and ventilating controls (2+2).
A. *Heater air control.*   C. *Heater fan switch.*
B. *Heater temperature*   D. *Heater outlet controls.*
control.

Fan Switch

The heater fan (C, Figs. 40 and 41) for the car heating and ventilating system considerably increases the flow of air through the system and is controlled by a three positions switch (marked "Fan").

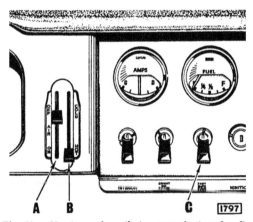

Fig. 41.   *Heating and ventilating controls. (not 2 + 2).*

Lift the switch to the second position for slow speed and to the third position for maximum speed, whichever is required.

Operation of the fan is required mainly when the car is stationary or running at a slow speed. At higher road speeds it will be found possible to dispense with the fan as air will be forced through the system due to the passage of the car through the air.

Cold Weather

To obtain fresh air heating, demisting and defrosting :

(a) Set fresh air control to DESIRED POSITION.

(b) Set temperature control to DE-SIRED POSITION.

(c) Switch ON fan at required speed.

(d) Open heater doors (2+2 cars, open outlets).

To obtain rapid demisting and defrosting :

(a) Turn fresh air control to FULLY ON.

(b) Set temperature control to HOT.

(c) Switch ON fan—FAST position.

(d) Close heater doors (2+2 cars, close outlets).

Warning

There is the possibility that fumes may be drawn into the car from the atmosphere when travelling in dense traffic and in such conditions it is advisable to close the heater air control and switch off the fan.

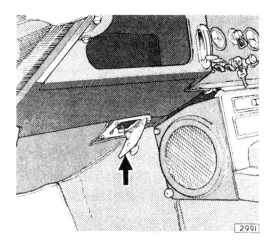

Fig. 42.   *Car interior heater doors.   (Open and fixed head coupe only).*

Hot Weather

To obtain ventilation and demisting :

- (a) Set fresh air control to DESIRED POSITION.
- (b) Set temperature control to COLD.
- (c) Switch ON fan at required speed.
- (d) Open heater doors (2+2 cars, open outlets).

To obtain rapid demisting:

- (a) Set fresh air control to FULLY ON.
- (b) Set temperature to COLD.
- (c) Switch ON fan—FAST position.
- (d) Close heater doors (2+2 cars, close outlets).

WINDSCREEN WASHING EQUIPMENT

The windscreen washer is electrically operated and comprises a plastic water container mounted in the engine compartment which is connected to jets at the base of the windscreen. Water is delivered to the jets by an electrically driven pump incorporated in the water container.

Operation

The windscreen washer should be used in conjunction with the windscreen wipers to remove foreign matter that settles on the windscreen.

Lift the switch lever (marked " Washer ") when the washer should operate immediately; release the switch when sufficient water has been delivered to the windscreen.

Warning

If the washer does not function immediately check that there is water in the container. The motor will be damaged if the switch is held pressed for more than one or two seconds if the water in the container is frozen.

The washer should not be used under freezing conditions as the fine jets of water spread over the windscreen by the blades will tend to freeze up.

In the summer the washer should be used freely to remove insects before they dry and harden on the screen.

Lucas 'Crystal Clear' Screenjet fluid may be added to the water to assist removal and to dissolve greasy smears from the glass.

Filling-up

The water should be absolutely CLEAN. If possible, use SOFT water for filling the container, but if this is not obtainable and hard water has to be used, frequent operation and occasional attention to the nozzle outlet holes will be amply repaid in preventing the formation of unwelcome deposits.

The correct water level is up to the bottom of the container neck. Do not overfill, or unnecessary splashing may result. Always replace the filler cover correctly after filling.

It is not possible to empty the container completely with the pump. Refilling is necessary when the water level has fallen below the level of the pump.

Do not continue to operate the switch after the available water has been used up otherwise damage may be caused to the unit.

Refilling the container will restore normal operation of the unit.

Keep the pump filter clean and the container free from sediment.

Cold Weather

The Lucas 5 S J windscreen washer container which is made of high density polythene can be given a safe degree of protection from frost damage down to $-28°F$ ($-33°C$) by the use of proprietary anti-freeze solvents as marketed by "TRICO" or as HOLTS "SCREENWASH".

Instruction regarding the solvent will be found on the container.

Denatured alcohol (Methylated Spirits) must NOT be used.

The use of this chemical will discolour the paintwork.

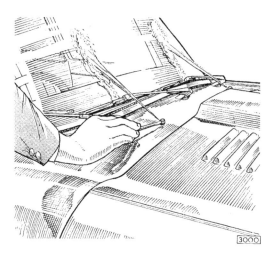

Fig. 44. *Adjusting the jets.*

Fig. 43. *The windscreen washer container is replenished through a hole in the cap.*

Adjusting the Jets

With the screwdriver turn the jet nozzle in the jet holder until the jets of water strike the windscreen in the area swept by the wiper blades. It may be necessary to adjust the nozzle slightly after a trial on the road due to jets of water being deflected by the air-stream.

Cleaning the Jet Nozzles

To clear a blocked jet nozzle completely unscrew the nozzle from the jet holder. Clear the small orifice with a piece of thin wire or blow out with compressed air; operate the washer with the nozzle removed. Allow the water to flush through the jet holder and then replace the nozzle.

49

LOWERING AND RAISING THE HOOD
(Open 2-seater Model)

To Lower the Hood

1. Release the three fasteners retaining the hood to the windscreen surround by pulling down the levers (Fig. 45).

2. Release the two hood rear retaining fasteners located inside the body at the rear of the doors (Fig. 46).

3. Lift the front of the hood and fold rearwards, *having first tilted the seats forward.*

4. Fold under the plastic rear window taking care that the window is lying flat without any creases in the material. Complete the folding of the hood, pull the top of the hood material rearwards and fold in the corners. Ensure that the hood material is not trapped in the hood mechanism (Fig. 47).

5. Collapse the frame and stow away at the rear of the seats.

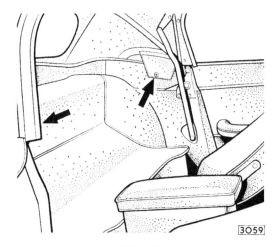

Fig. 46.

6. Pivot the two fastener straps secured to the header panel through 90°, pass the straps through the two holes in the header panel and fasten to the two outer snap fastener studs on the back panel (Fig. 48).

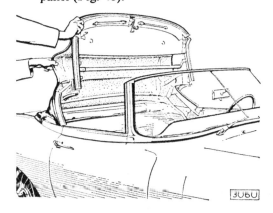

Fig. 47.

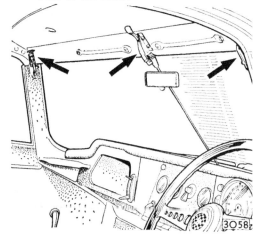

Fig. 45.

7. To fit the cover, place over the folded hood, pull down and fasten the three straps to the three fastener studs on the back panel. Snap the two side fasteners to the fastener studs located inside the body at the rear of the doors (Fig. 49).

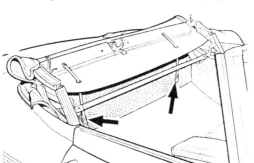

Fig. 48.

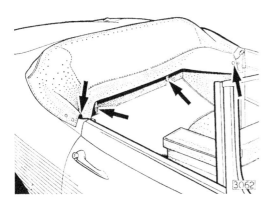

Fig. 49.

Pull the cover rearwards and clip the four hooks under the chromium beading strip (located at the rear of the hood) (Fig. 50).

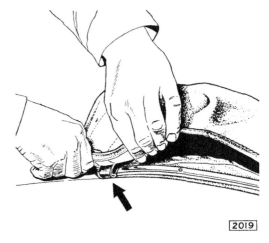

Fig. 50.

To Raise the Hood

1. Release the three straps, the two side snap fasteners and the four hook fasteners retaining the hood cover in position. Remove cover. Tilt seats forward.

2. Raise the hood and pull up to the windscreen surround.

3. Engage the catch hooks and pull up the levers.

4. Snap on the two fasteners located inside the body at the rear of the doors.

DETACHABLE HARDTOP

Fig. 51.   *Release clips above screen.*

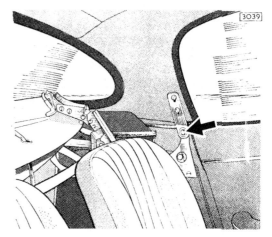

Fig. 52.   *Hardtop retaining bolts.*

To Remove the Hardtop :

1. Release the three fasteners retaining the hardtop to the windscreen surround by pulling down the levers (Fig. 51).

2. Lower the windows.

3. Remove the two retaining bolts and lift off (Fig. 52).

ROUTINE MAINTENANCE

This section deals with the lubrication and maintenance operations which require attention at regular intervals; the section is divided into the main components of the car and is sub-divided into the mileage at which the various maintenance operations should receive attention.

The importance of regular maintenance cannot be overstressed; the satisfactory running and high performance of which the car is capable is to a large extent dependent on the attention it receives. It is, therefore, recommended that careful attention is paid to the instructions detailed in this section and that servicing is carried out at the suggested periods.

The 1,000 mile (1,600 km.) Free Service

After the car has completed the first 1000 miles (1600 km.) a general check over should be carried out.

A Service Voucher is included in the literature wallet provided with the car and entitles the original owner to have the following servicing carried out by a Jaguar dealer free of charge, except for the cost of the lubricants used.

General test of car and making of any necessary minor adjustments.

Drain sump, renew oil filter, and seal and refill with new oil.

Drain gearbox and refill with new oil.

Check rear axle oil level.

Lubricate all grease nipples (excluding wheel bearings).

Check all hydraulic brake pipe unions and level of fluid in brake master cylinder reservoirs.

Check clutch pipe unions and level of fluid in clutch master cylinder reservoir.

(Not 2+2 Automatic Transmission).

Check tyre pressures.

Check front wheel alignment.

Check tightness of steering bolts and nuts.

Drain fluid in automatic transmission unit; wash oil pan; adjust front and rear bands and refill (2+2, if fitted).

Check tightness of front suspension bolts and nuts.

Check tightness of rear suspension bolts and nuts.

Check tightness of exhaust manifold flange nuts.

Tune up engine.

Tighten cylinder head nuts to correct torque figures.

The Service Voucher should be presented to the Jaguar Dealer by whom the car was supplied. Should the owner not reside in the vicinity of the original supplier or is temporarily absent when the service is required, the Voucher will be accepted by the nearest authorised Jaguar Dealer.

ENGINE

Daily

Checking the Engine Oil Level

Check the oil level with the car standing on level ground otherwise a false reading will be obtained.

Remove the dipstick and wipe it dry· Replace and withdraw the dipstick ; if the oil level is on the knurled patch, with the engine hot or cold, no additional oil is required. If the engine has been run immediately prior to making an oil level check, wait one minute after switching off before checking the oil level.

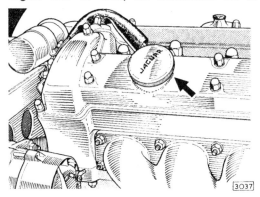

Fig. 53. *Engine oil filler.*

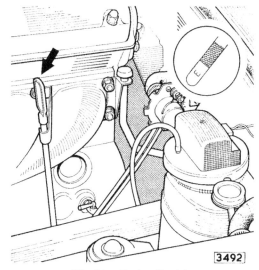

Fig. 54. *Engine dipstick.*

FUEL REQUIREMENTS FOR 9 TO 1 and 8 TO 1 COMPRESSION RATIO ENGINES

If the engine of your car is fitted with 9 to 1 compression ratio pistons (indicated by /9 after the engine number) use only Super grade fuel with a minimum octane rating of 98. (Research method.) If a car is fitted with 8 to 1 compression ratio pistons (indicated by /8 after the engine number) use premium grade fuel with a minimum rating of 94. (Research method.)

If, of necessity, the car has to be operated on lower octane fuel do not use full throttle otherwise detonation may occur with resultant piston trouble.

In the United Kingdom use '5 STAR' (9:1) or '4 STAR' (8:1) petrol.

Every 3,000 miles (5,000 km.)

Changing the Engine Oil

Note: Under certain adverse operating conditions, conducive to oil dilution and sludge formation, more frequent oil changing than the normal 3,000 mile (5,000 km.) period is advised. Where the car is used mainly for low-speed city driving, stop-start driving particularly in cold weather or in dusty territory the oil should be changed at least every 1,000 miles (1,600 km.).

The draining of the sump should be carried out at the end of a run when the oil is hot and therefore will flow more freely. The drain plug is situated at the right-hand rear corner of the sump. When the engine oil is changed, the oil filter which is situated on the right-hand side of the engine, must also be renewed.

First drain oil from the filter by removing the small hexagon-headed drain plug situated at the bottom of the filter head. Unscrew the central bolt and remove the canister and element. Thoroughly wash the canister in petrol and allow to dry out. When replacing the canister and element, renew the circular rubber seal in the filter head.

Note: Almost all modern engine oils contain special additives, and whilst it is permissible to mix the recommended brands it is undesirable. If it is desired to change from one brand to another this should be done when the sump is drained, and the Oil Company's recommendation in regard to flushing procedure should be followed.

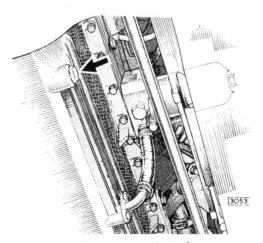

Fig. 55. *Engine drain plug.*

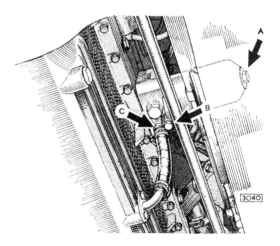

Fig. 56. *Engine oil filter—A, securing bolt; B, drain plug; C, oil pressure relief valve union.*

Distributor—Lubrication (Fig. 57)

Take care to prevent oil or grease from getting on or near the contact breaker points.

Remove the moulded cap at the top of the distributor by springing back the two clips. Lift off the rotor arm and apply a few drops of engine oil around the screw (A) now exposed. It is not necessary to remove the screw as it has clearance to permit the passage of oil.

Apply **one** drop of oil to the post (B) on which the contact breaker pivots. Lightly smear the cam (C) with grease. Lubricate the centrifugal advance mechanism by injecting a few drops of engine oil through the aperture at the edge of the contact breaker base plate.

Distributor Contact Breaker Points (Fig. 58)

Check the gap between the contact points with feeler gauges when the points are fully opened by one of the cams on the distributor shaft. A combined screwdriver and feeler gauge is provided in the tool kit.

The correct gap is .014″ - .016″ (.36mm. - .41mm.).

If the gap is incorrect, slacken (very slightly) the contact plate securing screw and adjust the gap by turning a screwdriver in the nick in the contact plate and the slot in the base plate, clockwise to decrease the gap and anti-clockwise to increase the gap. Tighten the securing screw and recheck the gap.

Examine the contact breaker points. If the contacts are burned or blackened, clean them with a fine carborundum stone or very fine emery cloth. Afterwards wipe away any trace of grease or metal dust with a petrol moistened cloth.

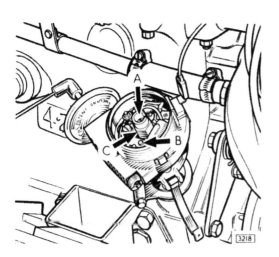

Fig. 57. *Distributor lubrication points.*

Fig. 58. *Checking the gap between the distributor contact points. The screw ' A ' secures the fixed contact plate; the contact gap is adjusted by turning a screwdriver in the slot ' B ' in the contact plate.*

Cleaning of the contacts is made easier if the contact breaker lever carrying the moving contact is removed. To do this, remove the nut, insulating piece and connections from the post to which the end of the contact breaker spring is anchored. The contact breaker lever can now be lifted off its pivot post.

Sparking Plugs

Every 3,000 miles (5,000 km.) or more often if operating conditions demand, withdraw, clean and reset the plugs.

The only efficient way to clean sparking plugs is to have them properly serviced on machines specially designed for this purpose. These machines operate with compressed air and utilise a dry abrasive material specially graded and selected to remove harmful deposits from the plug insulator without damaging the insulator surface. In addition the majority of the machines incorporate electrical testing apparatus enabling the plugs to be pressure tested to check their electrical efficiency and gas tightness.

The gap between the points should be .025" (.64 mm.). When adjusting the gap always move the side wire—never bend the centre wire.

The Champion Sparking Plug Co. supply a special combination gauge and setting tool, the use of which is recommended.

Every 12,000 miles (20,000 km.) a new set of plugs of the recommended type should be fitted. To save petrol and to ensure easy starting, the plugs should be cleaned and tested regularly.

Every 6,000 miles (10,000 km).

Water Pump and Alternator Drive Belt

The drive belt should be examined for wear periodically. Routine adjustment is not necessary as the drive belt is automatically adjusted by means of a spring loaded jockey pulley.

To remove the belt, release the top mounting bolt (B) in the alternator supporting strap (the nut is welded to the support bracket and cannot be turned). Release the bottom mounting nut (C) and swing the alternator inwards on bolt (A) to release the belt.

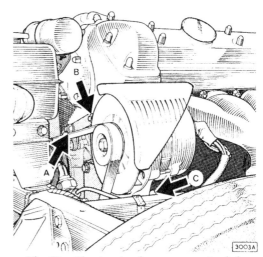

Fig. 59. *Showing the alternator mounting bolts.*

Oil Filter Element

It is most important to renew the oil filter element at every oil change.

To guard against the possibility of the filter being neglected to the extent where the element becomes completely choked, a balance valve is incorporated in the filter head which allows **unfiltered** oil to by-pass the element and reach bearings. This will be accompanied by a drop in the normal oil pressure of some 10 lb. per sq. in. and if this occurs the filter element should be renewed as soon as possible.

The oil filter is situated on the right-hand side of the engine and before removing the canister it will be necessary to drain the filter by removing the small hexagon-headed drain plug situated at the bottom of the filter head.

To gain access to the element, unscrew the central bolt when the canister complete with the element can be removed. Thoroughly wash out the canister with petrol and allow to dry before inserting the new element.

When replacing the canister renew the circular rubber seal in the filter head.

Top Timing Chain Tension

If the top timing chain is audible adjust the tension as follows :—

This operation requires the use of a special tool to enable the adjuster plate to be rotated. To gain access to the adjuster plate remove the breather housing attached to the front face of the cylinder head.

Slacken the locknut securing the serrated adjuster plate. Tension the chain by pressing the locking plunger inwards and rotating the adjuster plate in an anti-clockwise direction.

When correctly tensioned there should be slight flexibility on both outer sides of the chain below the camshaft sprockets, that is, the chain must not be dead tight. Release locking plunger, and securely tighten locknut. Refit the breather housing.

Every 12,000 miles (20,000 km.)

Air Cleaner

The air cleaner is of the paper element type and is situated in the engine compartment on the right-hand side adjacent to the carburetters.

No maintenance is necessary, but the element should be renewed every 12,000 miles (20,000 km.) or more frequently in dusty territories. To gain access to the element release the three spring clips retaining top cover to base. Remove two wing nuts attaching cleaner to air box and lift out element and cover. Remove serrated nut, and retainer plate from base of unit and withdraw element.

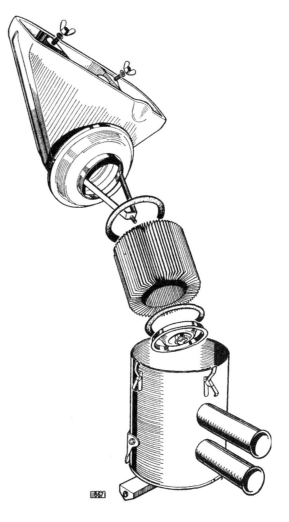

Fig. 60. *The air cleaner.*

CARBURETTERS AND FUEL SYSTEM
Every 3,000 miles (5,000 km.)

Lubricate Carburetter Piston Damper

Each carburetter is fitted with a hydraulic piston damper which unless periodically replenished with oil, will cause poor acceleration and spitting back through the carburetter on rapid opening of the throttle.

To replenish with oil, unscrew the cap on top of suction chambers and lift out the damper valve which is attached to the cap. Fill the hollow piston spindle, which can be seen down inside the bore of the suction chamber, with SAE 20 engine oil.

Checking Carburetter Slow Running

1. Cars fitted with synchromesh gearbox

The idling speed of the engine when fully warmed up should be set at 700 r.p.m.

Note: If the idling speed is less than 700 r.p.m. or if the engine is not idling smoothly, chatter from the constant mesh gears may be noticeable.

2. Cars fitted with automatic transmission (2+2)

The idling speed of the engine when fully warmed up should be set at 500 r.p.m. with P or N selected—There will be a slight reduction of idling speed when D1 or D2 is engaged.

If adjustment is required turn the three slow running volume screws (see Fig. 86) **by exactly equal amounts** until the idling speed observed on the revolution counter instrument, is correct.

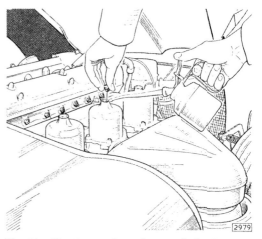

Fig. 61. *Topping up the carburetter hydraulic piston damper.*

Every 6,000 miles (10,000 km.)

Tune Carburetters

See instructions on page 65.

Cleaning Carburetter Filters

Removal of the bolt securing the petrol pipe banjo union to each float chamber will expose the filters. Remove the filters and clean in petrol; do not use a cloth as particles will stick to the gauze.

When refitting, insert the filter with the spring first and ensure that the fibre washers are replaced one to each side of the banjo union.

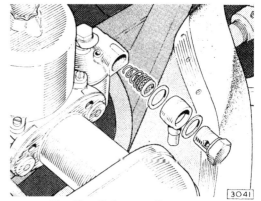

Fig. 62. *Carburetter filter removal.*

Fuel Feed Line Filter

The filter is attached to the bulkhead (right-hand side) and is of the glass bowl type with a flat filter gauze.

At the recommended intervals, or more frequently if the glass bowl shows signs of becoming full of sediment, slacken the locking nut, swing the retaining clip to one side and remove the bowl, sealing washer and filter gauze.

Clean the filter gauze and bowl by washing in petrol. Examine the sealing washer and if necessary fit a new one.

Fuel Pump

The fuel pump is located behind an access plate at the right hand side of the luggage compartment.

No periodic attention is required but if after long service the internal filter becomes choked it can only be due to excessive sediment in the fuel tank which should be removed and cleaned.

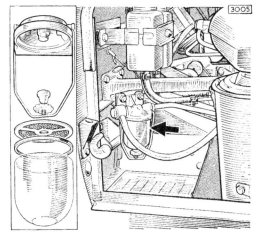

Fig. 63. *Fuel feed line filter.*

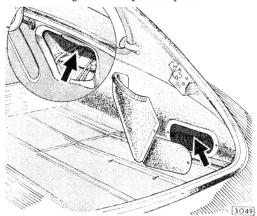

Fig. 64. *Location of petrol pump. (Fixed head coupe.) Inset shows location in Open 2-seater model.*

Every 12,000 miles (20,000 km.)

Fuel Tank Filter

The fuel tank filter is located within the drain plug tube on the underside of the fuel tank.

At the recommended intervals drain the fuel away into a clean container by removing the drain plug tube.

It will be advantageous to carry out this operation when the tank is low in fuel.

Remove the filter from the fuel pump inlet pipe by slackening the union nut and holding the filter, then unscrewing the filter.

Thoroughly clean the filter assembly in fuel, do not use cloth as particles may stick to the gauze.

Replace the drain plug tube sealing washer if damaged and refit the filter to the fuel pump inlet pipe. Always filter the fuel before returning to the tank.

COOLING SYSTEM

Daily

Checking Radiator Coolant Level

Every day check the level of the coolant in the radiator header tank and if necessary top up to the bottom of the filler neck.

Use water that is as soft as is procurable; hard water produces scale which in time will affect the cooling efficiency of the system.

Care must be taken when removing the filler cap if the engine is hot; it is advisable to protect the hands against escaping steam. Turn the cap slowly anti-clockwise until the resistance of the safety stop is felt. Leave the cap in this position until all pressure is released before removing completely.

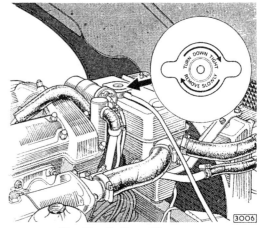

Fig. 65. *Radiator filler cap.*

Periodically

Care of the Cooling System

The entire cooling system should occasionally be flushed out to remove sediment. To do this, open the radiator block and cylinder block drain taps and insert a water hose into the radiator filler neck. Allow the water to flow through the system, with the engine running at a fast idle speed (1,000 r.p.m.) to cause circulation, until the water runs clear.

Since deposits in the water will in time cause fouling of the surfaces of the cooling system with consequent impaired efficiency it is desirable to retard this tendency as much as possible by using water as nearly neutral (soft) as is available. One of the approved brands of water inhibitor may be used with advantage to obviate the creation of deposits in the system.

Check the radiator water level after running the engine and top up if necessary.

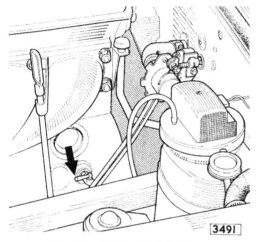

Fig. 66. *Cylinder block drain tap.*

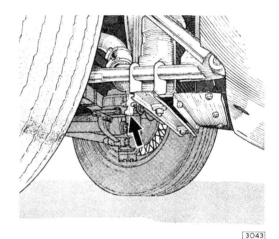

Fig. 67. *Radiator drain tap.*

Refilling the Cooling System—Important

When refilling the cooling system following complete drainage, place the heater temperature control in the 'Hot' position to allow the heater system to be filled with coolant. Re-check the level after running the engine for a short period.

CLUTCH
(Not 2+2 Automatic Transmission)
Weekly

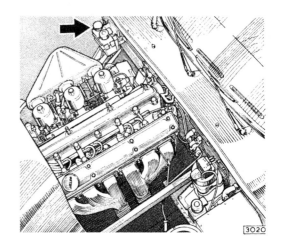

Clutch Fluid Level
Right-hand drive cars

The fluid reservoir for the hydraulically operated clutch is situated on the bulkhead (adjacent to the brake reservoir), on the driver's side, and it is important that the fluid does not fall below the level marked " Fluid Level ".

Fig. 68.   *Clutch fluid reservoir—right-hand drive.*

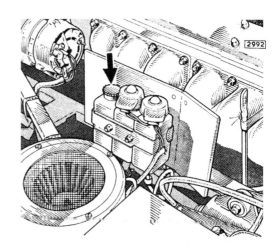

Left-hand drive cars

The fluid reservoir for the hydraulically operated clutch is situated on the exhaust manifold adjacent to the twin brake reservoirs.

Fig. 69.   *Clutch fluid reservoir—left-hand drive.*

GEARBOX

Every 3,000 miles (5,000 km.)

Gearbox Oil Level

Check the level of the oil in the gearbox with the car standing on level ground.

A combined level and filler plug is fitted on the left-hand side of the gearbox. Clean off any dirt from around the plug before removing it.

The level of the oil should be to the bottom of the filler and level plug hole.

The filler plug is accessible from inside the car through an aperture in the left-hand vertical face of the gearbox cowl. To obtain access to the plug remove the seat cushions, slide the seat rearwards to the full extent ; lift the front carpet and roll forward to expose the two snap fasteners retaining the gearbox cowl covering to the floor.

Release the snap fasteners and raise the panel. Remove the front aperture cover now

exposed and insert a tubular wrench through the aperture to remove the plug.

In the interests of cleanliness always cover the carpets before carrying out lubrication.

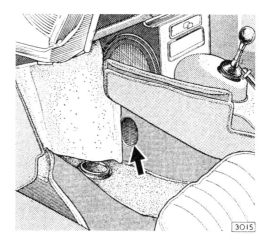

Fig. 70. *Showing the location of the gearbox level and filler plug aperture in the side of the gearbox cowl.*

Every 12,000 miles (20,000 km.)

Changing the Gearbox Oil

The draining of the gearbox should be carried out at the end of a run when the oil is hot and therefore will flow more freely. The drain plug is situated at the front end of the gearbox casing.

After all the oil has drained replace the drain plug and refill the gearbox with the recommended grade of oil through the combined filler and level plug hole situated on the left-hand side of the gearbox casing ; the level should be to the bottom of the hole.

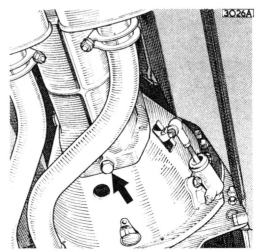

Fig. 71. *Gearbox drain plug.*

AUTOMATIC TRANSMISSION (2 + 2)

Every 3,000 miles (5,000 km.)

Check transmission fluid level.

The transmission filler tube and dipstick are located on the left-hand side of the engine adjacent to the engine oil dip-stick.

Before checking the fluid level, the car should be on level ground and the transmission should be at the normal operating temperature.

Set the handbrake and select P position.

The engine should be at normal idle.

While the engine is running, remove the dipstick, wipe clean and replace in the filler tube in its correct position.

Withdraw immediately and check.

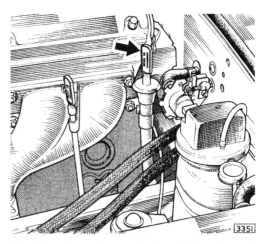

Fig. 72. *Automatic transmission oil filler tube and dipstick.*

If necessary, add fluid to bring the level to the FULL mark on the dipstick. The difference between FULL and LOW marks on the stick represents approximately $1\frac{1}{2}$ pints (2 U.S., pints or .75 litres).

Be careful not to overfill.

If fluid is checked with the transmission cold, a false reading will be obtained and filling to the FULL mark will cause it to be overfilled.

If it is found necessary to add fluid frequently it will be an indication that there is a leakage in the transmission and it should be investigated immediately to prevent damage to the transmission.

Every 21,000 miles (35,000 km.)

Fluid Changing and Band Adjustment

Drain the oil; remove the oil pan and wash out. Adjust the front and rear bands. Refit the oil pan and refill with oil.

Note: As the band adjustment requires the use of special tools, this operation is best entrusted to a Jaguar dealer.

RECOMMENDED LUBRICANTS

AUTOMATIC TRANSMISSION UNIT

MOBIL	CASTROL	SHELL	ESSO	B.P.	DUCKHAM	REGENT Caltex/Texaco
Mobilfluid 200	Castrol T.Q.	Shell Donax T.6	Esso Automatic Transmission Fluid	Automatic Transmission Fluid Type A	Nolmatic	Texamatic Fluid

PROPELLER SHAFT

The propeller shaft universal joints and sliding spline are of the 'sealed for life' type and require no periodic lubrication.

REAR AXLE
Every 3,000 miles (5,000 km.)

Checking Rear Axle Oil Level

Check the level of the oil in the rear axle with the car standing on level ground.

A combined filler and level plug is fitted in the rear of the axle casing accessible from underneath the car. Clean off any dirt from around the plug before removing it.

The level of the oil should be to the bottom of the filler and level plug hole ; use only HYPOID oil of the correct grade and since different brands may not mix satisfactorily, draining and refilling is preferable to replenishing if the brand of oil in the axle is unknown.

Rear Axle Half Shafts

The two rear axle half shafts are fitted with 'sealed for life' universal joints and do not require periodic lubrication.

Fig. 73. *Rear axle filler and level plug*

Every 12,000 miles (20,000 km.)

Changing the Rear Axle Oil

The draining of the rear axle should be carried out at the end of a run when the oil is hot and will therefore flow more freely. The drain plug is situated in the base of the differential casing.

After the oil has drained, replace the drain plug and refill the rear axle with the recommended grade of oil after removal of the combined filler and level plug situated in rear cover.

The level of the oil should be to the bottom of the filler and level plug hole when the car is standing on level ground.

Use only HYPOID oil of the correct grade.

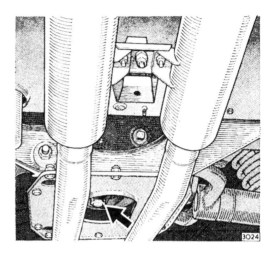

Fig. 74.   *Rear axle drain plug*

Rear Axle—Oil Changing

Do NOT drain and refill the rear axle at the first 1,000 mile (1,600 km.) free service. Change the rear axle oil after the car has completed 6,000 miles (10,000 km.) and thereafter at the recommended intervals.

FRONT SUSPENSION AND STEERING

Front Suspension

The front suspension wishbone levers and anti-roll bar are supported in rubber bushes which do not require any attention.

Front Shock Absorbers

The front shock absorbers are of the telescopic type and no replenishment with fluid is necessary or provided for.

Every 6,000 miles (10,000 km.)

Steering Housing

The steering gear is of the rack and pinion type and is attached to the front cross member of the frame assembly. A grease nipple for the lubrication of the rack and pinion housing is accessible from underneath the front of the car from the driver's side.

Do not over lubricate the steering housing to the extent where the rubber bellows at the end of the housing becomes distended. Check that the clips at the ends of the bellows are fully tightened otherwise the grease will escape from the housing.

Steering Tie-rods

Lubricate the ball joints of the two steering tie-rods with the recommended lubricant. A bleed hole is provided in each ball joint; the hole is covered by a nylon washer which lifts under pressure and indicates when sufficient lubricant has been applied. When carrying out this operation examine the rubber seals at the bottom of the ball housing to see if they have become displaced or split. In this event they should be repositioned or replaced as any dirt or water that enters the joint will cause premature wear.

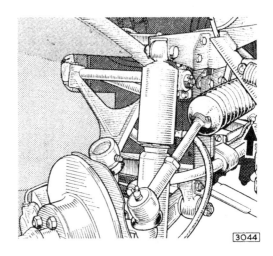

Fig. 75. *Steering housing grease nipples.*

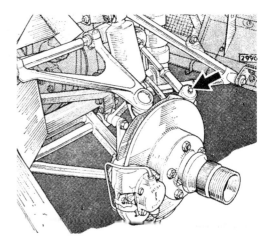

Fig. 76. *Steering tie-rod grease nipple.*

Wheel Swivels

Lubricate the nipples (four per car) fitted to the top and bottom of the wheel swivels.

A bleed hole is provided in each ball joint ; the hole is covered by a nylon washer which lifts under pressure and indicates when sufficient lubricant has been applied.

The nipples are accessible from underneath the front of the car.

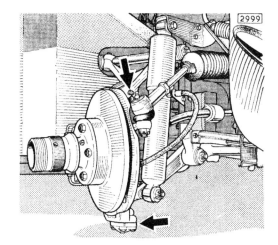

Fig. 77. *Steering swivel grease nipples.*

Every 6,000 miles (10,000 km.)

Front Wheel Alignment

As this operation requires the use of special tools it is best entrusted to a Jaguar dealer.

REAR SUSPENSION

Rear Springs

The rear suspension is by coil springs which do not require maintenance attention.

Rear Shock Absorbers

The rear shock absorbers are of the telescopic type and no replenishment with fluid is necessary or provided for

Every 6,000 miles (10,000 km.)

Outer Pivot Bearings

A grease nipple is located in the centre of the rear wishbone outer pivot. Lubricate sparingly with the recommended grade of lubricant. A bleed hole is provided, opposite the grease nipple, to indicate when an excess of lubricant has been applied. Always ascertain that the bleed hole is clear before carrying out operation.

Inner Pivot Bearing

Two grease nipples are provided located at either end of the wishbone fork. Lubricate sparingly with the recommended grade of lubricant.

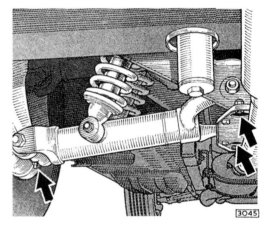

Fig. 78. *Outer and inner pivot bearing grease nipples*

WHEEL BEARINGS

Every 12,000 miles (20,000 km.)

Rear Wheel Bearings

A hole in the hub bearing housing for lubrication of the wheel bearings is accessible after removal of the wheel. Clean off the area around the dust cap to ensure that no dirt enters the hub. Prise out the cap and inject the recommended grade of grease through the hole until no more will enter. If a pressure gun is used take care not to build-up pressure in the hub as the grease may escape past the oil seal. Refit the dust cap.

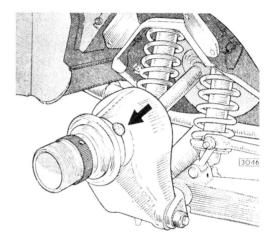

Fig. 79.   *Rear wheel hub bearing grease cap.*

Front Wheel Bearings

Removal of the wheels will expose a grease nipple in the wheel bearing hubs. Lubricate sparingly with the recommended grade of lubricant. If excess grease is pumped into the bearing hubs the grease will exude into the bore of the splined hubs. Always thoroughly clean the grease nipple before applying the grease gun.

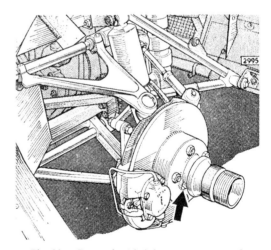

Fig. 80.   *Front wheel hub bearing grease nipple.*

BRAKING SYSTEM

Weekly

Brake Fluid Level

On right-hand drive cars the fluid reservoirs (two) for the hydraulic brakes are attached to the bulkhead.

On left-hand drive cars the fluid reservoirs (two) for the hydraulic brakes are attached adjacent to the exhaust manifold.

The reservoir to the master cylinder feeds the rear brakes and the reservoir to the servo feeds the front brakes.

At the recommended intervals check the level of fluid in the reservoir and top up if necessary to the level mark, above fixing strap, marked " Fluid Level " using only the correct specification of Brake Fluid.

Do NOT overfill.

The level can be plainly seen through the plastic reservoir container.

First, disconnect the two electrical cables from the " snap-on " terminals. Unscrew the filler cap and " top-up " if necessary to the recommended level. Insert the combined filler cap and float slowly into the reservoir to allow for displacement of fluid and screw down the cap. Wipe off any fluid from the top of the cap and connect the cables to either of the two terminals.

Note: A further indication that the fluid level is becoming low is provided by an indicator pin situated between the two terminals.

First press down the pin and allow it to return to its normal position ; if the pin can then be lifted with the thumb and forefinger the reservoir requires topping-up immediately.

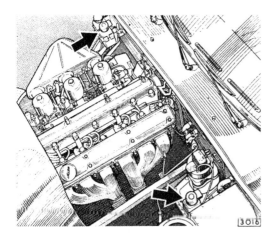

Fig. 81. *Brake fluid reservoirs—right-hand drive.*

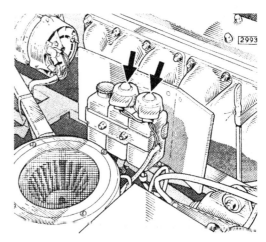

Fig. 82. *Brake fluid reservoirs—left-hand drive.*

Brake Fluid Level Warning Light

A warning light (marked " Brake Fluid—Handbrake ") situated on the facia behind the steering wheel, serves to indicate if the level in one or both of the brake fluid reservoirs has become low, provided the ignition is " on ". As the warning light is also illuminated when the handbrake is applied, the handbrake must be fully released before it is assumed that the fluid level is low. If with the ignition " on " and the handbrake fully released the warning light is illuminated the brake fluid must be " topped-up " immediately.

As the warning light is illuminated when the handbrake is applied and the ignition is " on " a two-fold purpose is served. Firstly, to avoid the possibility of driving away with the handbrake applied. Secondly, as a check that the warning light bulb has not " blown " ; if on first starting up the car with the handbrake fully applied, the warning light does not become illuminated the bulb should be changed immediately.

Note: If it is found that the fluid level falls rapidly indicating a leak from the system, the car should be taken immediately to the nearest Jaguar Dealer for examination.

Every 3,000 miles (5,000 km.)

Footbrake Adjustment

Both the front wheel and rear wheel brakes are so designed that no manual adjustment to compensate for brake friction pad wear is necessary as this automatically takes place when the footbrake is applied.

Handbrakes

The mechanically operated handbrakes are attached to the rear caliper bodies but form an independent mechanically actuated system carrying its own friction pads. The handbrakes are self adjusting to compensate for friction pad wear and automatically provide the necessary clearance between the friction pads and the discs.

If the travel of the handbrake lever is excessive the handbrake cable should be adjusted as follows :—

Handbrake Cable Adjustment

Fully release the handbrake lever in the car. Slacken the locknut at the rear end of the handbrake cable.

Adjust the length of the cable by screwing out the threaded adaptor to a point just short of where the handbrake operating levers at the calipers start to move. Check the adjustment by pressing each operating lever at the same time towards the caliper ; if any appreciable movement of the compensator linkage takes place the cable is too tight.

When correctly adjusted a certain amount of slackness will be apparent in the cable ; no attempt should be made to place the cable under tension or the handbrakes may bind.

Fig. 83.   Handbrake cable adjustment.

Every 6,000 miles (10,000 km.)

Friction Pads—Examination for Wear

At the recommended intervals, or if a loss of braking efficiency is noticed, the brake friction pads (2 per brake) should be examined for wear ; the ends of the pads can be easily observed through the apertures in the brake caliper. When the friction pads have worn down to a thickness of approximately $\frac{1}{4}''$ (7 mm.) they need renewing.

Friction Pads—Renewal

To remove the friction pads, unscrew the nut from the bolt attaching the friction pad retainer to the caliper and extract the bolt. Withdraw the pad retainer.

Insert a hooked implement through the hole in the metal tag attached to the friction pad and withdraw the pad by pulling on the tag.

To enable the new friction pads to be fitted it will be necessary to force the pistons back into the cylinder blocks by means of a special tool.

When all the new friction pads have been fitted, top up the supply tank to the recommended level.

Insert the new friction pads into the caliper ensuring that the slot in the metal plate attached to each pad engages with the button in the centre of the piston.

Finally, refit the friction pad retainer and secure with the bolt and nut. Apply the footbrake a few times to operate the self-adjusting mechanism, so that normal travel of the pedal is obtained.

Fig. 84. *Location of rear brake calipers.*

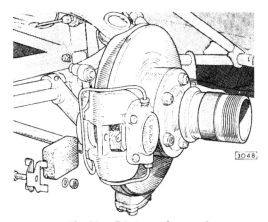

Fig. 85. *Friction pad removal.*

WHEELS AND TYRES

Weekly

Tyre Pressures

It is important to maintain the tyre pressures at the correct figures given on page 10 of this book. Incorrect pressures will affect the steering, riding comfort and tyre wear.

Check the inflation pressures when the tyres are cold and not when they have attained their normal running temperature ; tyre pressures increase with driving and any such increase should be ignored. Always ensure that the caps are fitted to the ends of the valves as they prevent the ingress of dirt and form a secondary seal to the valve core.

Tyre Replacement and Wheel Interchanging

When replacement of the rear tyres becomes necessary, fit new tyres to the existing rear wheels and, after balancing, fit these wheels to the front wheel positions on the car, fitting the existing front wheel and tyre assemblies (which should have useful tread life left) to the rear wheel positions on the car.

If at the time this operation is carried out the tyre of the spare wheel is in new condition, it can be fitted to one of the front wheel positions in preference to replacing one of the original rear tyres, which wheel and tyre then become the spare.

Note: Due to the change in the steering characteristics which can be introduced by fitting to the front wheel positions wheels and tyres which have been used on the rear wheel positions, interchanging of part worn tyres from rear to front wheel positions is not recommended.

Wheels and Tyres for Competition Use

Wheels

Note that chrome-plated wheels are not recommended for use on cars which will be participating in serious competition work.

If it is desired to use 6.50 × 15 Road Racing tyres on the rear wheels for competition purposes, these tyres must be fitted to special wheels (Part No. C.18922) having a wider rim section and revised spoking, which maintains the normal clearance between the tyre and the wheel arch panel and results in the rear track being increased.

These special rear wheels must in no circumstances be used in the front wheel position on the " E " Type car. Also note that, since these wheels are recommended only for competition use, they will not be supplied chromium plated. Special rear wheels (Part No. C.18922) will be supplied only as spares and NOT as part of the specification of a new car.

It is recommended that, prior to and following participation in competition events covering racing or rallies, the wheels are checked to ensure that they are in an undamaged condition, are running true and that the spokes are correctly tensioned.

It is not desirable that Road Racing tyres should be fitted to cars which will be used only on the road.

Racing Tyres

6.00 × 15 Dunlop R.5 Road Racing tyres should be fitted if "E" Type cars are being raced. If it is desired to fit larger section rear tyres to reduce the possibility of wheel spin under full power acceleration or to adjust the gear ratio, 6.50 × 15 Dunlop R.5 Road Racing tyres can be fitted, but only if these tyres are fitted on the special rear wheels described above.

Note that it is not desirable that cars should be run under normal touring conditions using Dunlop R.5 Road Racing tyres since, although these tyres give the best handling qualities under racing conditions, they do not have the same qualities for touring purposes as the Road Speed tyre, in addition to which the tyre walls are more liable to damage through kerbing.

Tyre Pressures for Racing

Recommended tyre pressures for racing purposes are :—

45 p.s.i. front and rear, Cold
(3.2 kg./cm.^{2})

Dependent upon temperature and maximum speed conditions these pressures should be raised to :

50 p.s.i. front and rear, Cold
(3.5 kg./ cm.^{2})

The minimum tyre pressures for Dunlop R.5 Road Racing tyres if used for normal touring purposes are :

30 p.s.i. front and rear, Cold
(2.1 kg./cm^2.)

Owners who wish to obtain supplies of Dunlop R.5 Road Racing tyres should, if resident in the United Kingdom, contact the Dunlop Rubber Company Limited, Racing Division, Fort Dunlop, Erdington, Birmingham 24. Owners resident outside the United Kingdom should obtain their requirements through contact with the head office of The Dunlop Organisation in the country concerned.

COACHWORK
Every 6,000 miles (10,000 km.)

Door Drain Holes

At the recommended intervals clear the drain holes in the bottom of the doors with a piece of stiff wire.

Periodically

Carpets

These may be cleaned by brushing or with a vacuum cleaner. Grease or oil stains can be removed with petrol.

Chromium Plate

Whilst all chrome-plated parts used on Jaguar cars are produced to a high standard, owners should note that deterioration of the plate may occur unless regular maintenance treatment is given.

With cars that are washed frequently and not operated in areas where climatic conditions liable to effect chrome plate exist, normal washing and leathering of the chrome and occasional use of chrome polish will maintain the plate in satisfactory condition.

In certain industrial areas or coastal areas, however, discolouration of the chrome plate from deposits in the atmosphere is liable to occur and more frequent attention is required.

Particular attention is drawn to the fact that salt is now commonly used on roads for frost or snow dispersal and it is of great importance that in areas where this treatment is used cars should be washed off as quickly as possible following use under these conditions.

Hood—Open 2 Seater

When cleaning the hood material care must be taken not to destroy the water-proofing qualities. Cleaning may be carried out with a soft brush and a " frothy " solution of a neutral soap and water. Stains may be removed by rubbing lightly with a white cloth moistened in carbon tetrachloride or methylated spirits.

Do not rub the plastic rear window with a dry cloth. Wash with soap and water only and rinse with clean water ; dry with a soft cloth or sponge.

Head Lining—Fixed Head Coupe

Dirt may be removed from the lining by the use of a vacuum cleaner. Stains may be removed by means of a white cloth moistened with carbon tetrachloride or methylated spirit applied briskly but without pressure.

Paintwork

Never clean the paintwork other than by washing with a soft sponge and hose pipe. Use a steady flow of water and sponge lightly. Dry and polish the paintwork with a good quality wash leather.

Tar may be removed with a clean soft cloth moistened with petrol or with a proprietary brand of tar remover.

The paintwork may be polished from time to time with a good quality proprietary polish, either wax or emulsion type.

Upholstery

The leather should be wiped over occasionally with a cloth damped in warm soapy water. Repeat operation using fresh cloth and water alone (avoid flooding the leather) and finish by drying and polishing with a soft dry cloth. It is important to use a mild, non-caustic soap of the toilet kind and to avoid the use of petrol and detergents.

OIL CAN LUBRICATION

Every 6,000 miles (10,000 km.)

At the recommended intervals carry out oil can lubrication of the following points :

Seat runner and adjusting mechanism.
Handbrake lever ratchet.
Door locks.

Luggage compartment hinges and catches.
Bonnet hinges and catches.
Windscreen wiper arms.
Accelerator and carburetter linkage.
Fuel filler cover hinge.

ELECTRICAL EQUIPMENT

Monthly

Battery Electrolyte level

At the recommended intervals examine the electrolyte level in the battery cells, and top up if necessary with distilled water until the separators are just covered. Under no circumstances overfill above this level. Never use tap water to " top-up " the battery as the impurities in the water will be harmful to the plates.

Battery Connections

At the time of checking the electrolyte level ensure that battery terminals are clean and tight : if corroded, clean the insides of the terminals and smear with petroleum jelly.

IMPORTANT

These cars have a Negative Earth (ground) system and certain of the electrical components are different to those fitted to positive earth cars. When fitting auxiliary equipment or replacing any of the electrical components use only those specified for this particular model or ensure that they are suitable for use with negative earth.

RECOMMENDED HYDRAULIC FLUID

Braking System and Clutch Operation

Castrol/Girling Crimson Clutch/Brake Fluid is recommended. This conforms to S.A.E. 70 R3 specification modified for additional safety to give a higher boiling point.

Where this is not available, only fluid guaranteed to conform to S.A.E. 70 R3 specification, may be used as an alternative after draining the system and flushing.

For competition use (Races or Rallies): Castrol/Girling Disc Brake Racing Fluid (coloured amber).

RECOMMENDED LUBRICANTS

Component	MOBIL	CASTROL	SHELL	ESSO	B.P.	DUCKHAM	REGENT Caltex/Texaco
Engine	Mobiloil Special*	Castrol XL 20W/50	Shell Super Oil	Esso Extra Motor Oil 10/W30* Esso Extra Motor Oil 20W/40	Super Visco-Static 10W/40	Q20-50 or Q5500*	Havoline 20W/40 or 10W/30*
Upper cylinder lubrication	Mobil Upperlube	Castrollo	Shell U.C.L. or Donax U.	Esso U.C.L.	U.C.L.	Adcoid Liquid	Regent U.C.L.
Distributor oil can points / Oil can lubrication	Mobiloil A	Castrol XL	Shell X-100 30	Esso Motor Oil 20W/30	Energol SAE 30	NOL 30	Havoline 30
Gearbox / Rear axle	Mobilube GX 90	Castrol Hypoy	Spirax 90 E.P.	Esso Gear Oil GP 90/140	Gear Oil SAE 90 E.P.	Hypoid 90	Multigear Lubricant EP90
Front wheel bearings / Rear wheel bearings / Distributor cam / Steering rack housing	Mobilgrease MP	Castrolease LM	Retinax A	Esso Multi-purpose Grease H	Energrease L.2	LB 10	Marfak All Purpose
Steering tie-rods / Wheel swivels / Door hinges / Rear wishbone pivots	Mobilgrease MP	Castrolease LM	Retinax A	Esso Multi-purpose Grease H	Energrease L.2	LB 10	Marfak All Purpose
Automatic transmission unit	Mobil Fluid 200	Castrol T.Q.	Shell Donax T6	Esso Automatic Transmission Fluid	Automatic Transmission Fluid Type A	Nolmatic	Texamatic Fluid

* These oils should NOT be used in worn engines requiring overhaul. If an SAE 30 or 40 oil has previously been used in the engine a slight increase in oil consumption may be noticed but this will be compensated by the advantages gained.

SUMMARY OF MAINTENANCE

Daily

Check radiator water level.
Check engine oil level.

Weekly

Check tyre pressures (including spare wheel).

Monthly

Check battery electrolyte level and connections.

Every 3,000 miles (5,000 km.)

Check radiator water level.
Check tyre pressures (including spare wheel).
Check battery electrolyte level and connections.
Check fluid level in brake and clutch master cylinder reservoirs.
Check gearbox oil level.
Check rear axle oil level.
Drain engine sump and refill.
Renew oil filter element and seal.
Top up carburetter hydraulic piston dampers.
Lubricate distributor & check contact points.
Clean, adjust and test sparking plugs.
Check carburetter slow running.
Check fluid level in automatic transmission unit (2+2, if fitted).

Every 6,000 miles (10,000 km.)

Carry out 3,000 mile (5,000 km.) service
Lubricate all grease nipples (excluding wheel bearings).

Renew oil filter element and seal.
Tune carburetters.
Examine brake friction pads for wear.
Clear drain holes in bottoms of doors.
Adjust top timing chain (if necessary).
Check front wheel alignment.
Check alternator belt for wear.
Carry out oil can lubrication of (a) seat runner and adjusting mechanism, (b) handbrake lever ratchet, (c) door locks, (d) luggage compartment hinges and catches, (e) bonnet hinges and catches, (f) windscreen wiper arms, (g) accelerator and carburetter linkage, (h) fuel filler cover hinge.

Every 12,000 miles (20,000 km.)

Carry out 3,000 mile and 6,000 mile (5,000 and 10,000 km.) service.
Drain and refill gearbox.
Drain and refill rear axle.
Renew air cleaner element.
Renew sparking plugs.
Lubricate front and rear wheel hub bearings.
Check front and rear wheel bearings for end float (additional charge for adjustment).
Check exhaust system for leaks.
Check and tighten all chassis and body nuts, bolts and screws.
Check headlamp alignment and adjust as necessary.

Every 21,000 miles (35,000 km.)

Carry out 3,000 mile (5,000 km.) service
Drain automatic transmission unit; wash out oil pan. Adjust front and rear bands and refill unit.

SERVICE INSTRUCTIONS

This section deals with certain operations which although not requiring attention at regular intervals, may be found necessary either due to the mileage covered or to the replacement of parts.

Normally these operations should be undertaken by a Jaguar Distributor or Dealer but the instructions are included as a guide for the enthusiast or the owner living in a remote district.

CARBURETTER TUNING

It is useless to attempt carburetter tuning until the cylinder compressions, valve clearances, sparking plug gaps and contact breaker point gaps have been tested, checked and adjusted, if necessary. The distributor centrifugal advance mechanism and vacuum advance operation should be checked and ignition timing set to the figure given under " General Data ", with the centrifugal advance and vacuum advance mechanisms in the static position. For final road test, adjustment of not more than six clicks of the micrometer adjustment at the distributor to either advance or retard is permitted. The ignition setting is important since if retarded or advanced too far the setting of the carburetters will be affected. As the needle size is determined during engine development, tuning of the carburetters is confined to the correct idling setting.

Tuning

The air intake should be removed and the engine run until it has attained its normal operating temperature. Release the three pinch bolts securing the two piece throttle levers to the carburetter throttle spindles.

Taking one carburetter at a time close each throttle butterfly valve fully by rotating the throttle spindle in a clockwise direction looking from the front; with the throttle held closed tighten the pinch bolt keeping the two piece throttle lever in the midway position.

Repeat for the other two carburetters, then operate the accelerator linkage and observe if all the throttles are opening simultaneously by noting the movement of the full throttle stops at the left-hand side of the throttle spindles.

Note: On initial movement of the accelerator linkage there should be a limited amount of lost motion at the throttle spindles; this ensures that all the throttle butterfly valves can return to the fully closed position.

Screw down the slow running volume screws (A, Fig. 86) on to their seatings and then unscrew 2 full turns. Remove the piston and suction chambers ; disconnect the jet control linkage by removing the clevis pins from the connecting rod fork ends underneath the front and rear carburetters. Unscrew the mixture adjusting screws (C) until each jet is flush with the bridge of its carburetter. Replace the pistons and suction chambers and check that each piston falls freely on to the bridge of its carburetter (by means of the piston lifting pin). Turn down the mixture adjusting screws 2½ turns.

Restart the engine and adjust to the desired idling speed of 700 r.p.m. (500 r.p.m. automatic transmission) by moving each slow running volume screw an equal amount. By listening to the hiss in the intakes, adjust the slow running screws until the intensity of the hiss is similar on all intakes. This will synchronise the mixture flow of the three carburetters.

When this is satisfactory the mixture should be adjusted by screwing all the mixture adjusting screws up (weaker) or down (richer) by the same amount until the

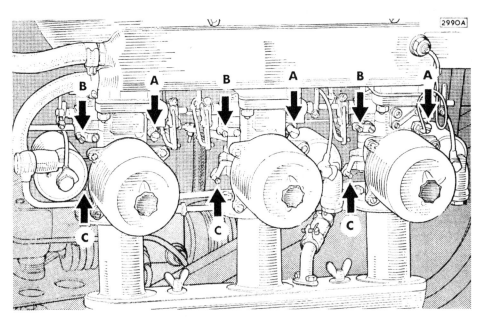

Fig. 86. *Carburetter tuning.*

A—Slow running volume screw.   *B—Fast idle screw.*
C—Mixture adjusting screw.

86

fastest idling speed is obtained consistent with even firing.

As the mixture is adjusted, the engine will probably run faster and it may therefore be necessary to screw down the slow running volume screws in order to reduce the speed.

Now check the mixture strength by lifting the piston of the front carburetter by approximately $\frac{1}{32}''$ (.8 mm.) when, if :

(a) the engine speed increases and **continues to run faster,** this indicates that the mixture is too rich.

(b) the engine speed immediately decreases, this indicates that the mixture is too weak.

(c) the engine speed **momentarily** increases very slightly, this indicates that the mixture is correct.

Repeat the operation at the remaining two carburetters and after adjustment recheck the front carburetter since the carburetters are interdependent.

When the mixture is correct, the exhaust note should be regular and even. If it is irregular with a splashy type of misfire and colourless exhaust, the mixture is too weak. If there is a regular or rhythmical type of misfire in the exhaust beat together with a blackish exhaust, then the mixture is too rich.

When reconnecting the jet operating cable allow $\frac{1}{16}''$ (1.5 mm.) free travel at the bottom of the facia panel control before the jet levers begin to move.

Fast Idle Setting

Set the mixture control knob on the facia panel to the highest position in the slide immediately short of the position where the mixture adjusting screw levers (C) begin to move. This will be approaching the mid-travel position of the control knob and approximates to $\frac{5}{8}''$ (16 mm.) movement at the bottom of the jet levers. Adjust the fast idle screws (B) on the throttle stops to give an engine speed of about 1,000 r.p.m. (when hot).

IGNITION TIMING

Set the micrometer adjustment in the centre of the scale.

Rotate the engine until the rotor-arm approaches the No. 6 (front) cylinder segment in the distributor cap.

Slowly rotate the engine until the ignition timing scale on the crankshaft damper is the appropriate number of degrees (see " Data ") before the pointer on the sump.

Connect a 12 volt test lamp with one lead to the distributor terminal (or the CB terminal of the ignition coil) and the other to a good earth.

Slacken the distributor clamping plate pinch bolt. Switch on the ignition.

Slowly rotate the distributor body until the points are just breaking, that is, when the lamp lights up.

Tighten the distributor plate pinch bolt.

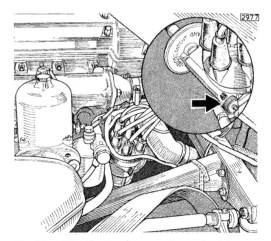

Fig. 87. *Distributor advance and retard mechanism.*

A maximum of six clicks on the vernier adjustment from this setting, to either advance or retard, is allowed.

FRONT WHEEL CAMBER ANGLE—ADJUSTMENT

Special links should be used when setting the camber angle of the front wheels. These links, which fit over the nuts securing the shock absorbers at top and bottom, hold the suspension in the mid-laden position. If the links are not available, additional weight should be added to the car to give a dimension of $13\frac{1}{2}''$ (34.29 cm.) between the centres of the shock absorber mountings which will be the mid-laden point of the front suspension.

Ensure that the tyre pressures are correct and that the car is standing on a level surface.

Camber Angle ($\frac{1}{4}° \pm \frac{1}{2}°$) positive.

Note: The camber angle for each wheel must not vary by more than $\frac{1}{2}°$.

Line up the front wheel being checked parallel to the centre line of the car. Using an approved gauge, check the camber angle. Rotate the wheel being checked through 180° and re-check.

Adjustment is effected by removing or adding shims between the front suspension top wishbone bracket and the frame member.

When removing or adding shims note that the top holes in the shims are slotted and the bolts need only be slackened off; the bottom holes are not slotted and it is necessary therefore to remove the fixing bolts completely.

Inserting shims increases positive camber; removing shims increases negative camber or decreases positive camber. Remove or add an equal thickness of shims from each position, otherwise the castor angle will be affected. It should be noted that $\frac{1}{16}''$ (1.6 mm.) of shimming will alter the camber angle by approximately $\frac{1}{4}°$.

Check the other front wheel in a similar manner. If any adjustment is made to the

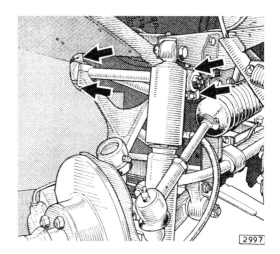

Fig. 88. *The front wheel camber angle is adjusted by means of the shims indicated by arrows. Remove or add an equal thickness of shims from each position.*

camber angle, the front wheel alignment should be checked and if necessary be re-set (see page 71).

REAR WHEEL CAMBER ANGLE—ADJUSTMENT

Owing to the variations in camber angle with different suspension heights, it is necessary to lock the rear suspension in the mid-laden position by means of two setting links. These links fit over the hub carrier fulcrum nut and hook into the lower hole of the rear mounting. If the links are not available, place weights in the boot of the car to load the suspension so that a dimension taken from the the lower hole of the rear mounting to the centre of the hub carrier fulcrum nut is 8.$\frac{3}{16}''$ (20.79 cm.) This will be the mid-laden point of the rear suspension.

Ensure that the car tyre pressures are correct and that the car is standing on level ground. Roll the car forward 3 lengths.

Using an approved gauge check the camber angle.

Camber angle. $\frac{3}{4}° \pm \frac{1}{4}°$ negative.

Roll car forward 3 lengths and re-check.

Note: The camber angle for each wheel must not vary by more than $\frac{1}{4}°$.

Adjustment is effected by removing or adding shims between rear half shaft inboard universal joint and brake disc.

To adjust proceed as follows :—

Jack up the car and remove wheel being checked. Remove the four bolts and nuts securing the rear half shaft universal joint flange to the brake disc. Break away joint and add or subtract shims as necessary. Refit joint and fully tighten bolts and nuts. Adjust other wheel in a similar manner. Refit and lower wheels and remove jack.

Roll car forward three lengths and re-

Fig. 89. *The rear wheel camber angle is adjusted by means of shims indicated by the arrow.*

check camber angle.

It should be noted that one shim .020″ (0.5 mm.) will alter camber angle by approximately $\frac{1}{4}°$.

CASTOR ANGLE—ADJUSTMENT

Special links should be used when setting the castor angle of the front wheels. These links, which fit over the nuts of the top and bottom shock absorber mountings, hold the suspension in the mid-laden position position. If the links are not available, additional weight should be added to the car to give a dimension of 13½" (34.28 cm.) between the centres of the shock absorber mountings which will be the mid-laden point of the front suspension.

Ensure that the tyre pressures are correct and that the car is standing on a level surface.

Using an approved gauge check the castor angle.

Castor Angle. $2° \pm \frac{1}{2}°$ positive.

Note: The castor angle for each wheel must not vary by more than $\frac{1}{2}°$.

Adjustment is effected by rotating the round threaded shaft on the front suspension top wishbone bracket.

Remove split pins and release nuts situated at the front and rear of shaft and release wishbone bracket clamping bolts. Shaft may now be turned with spanner placed on the two flats provided on shaft.

Note. It is essential that split pins be removed and nuts released from shaft otherwise a strain will be placed on the rubber mounting bushes.

To increase positive castor angle rotate shaft anti-clockwise (viewed from front of car); to decrease positive castor angle rotate shaft clockwise. After adjustment re-tighten clamp bolts (two) re-tighten nuts and fit split pins.

If any adjustment is made to the castor angle, the front wheel alignment should be checked and if necessary re-set (see page 71).

The front of the car should be jacked up when turning the wheels from lock to lock during checking.

Fig. 90. *The castor angle is adjusted by rotating the shaft indicated by the arrow.*

BLEEDING THE BRAKE HYDRAULIC SYSTEM

" Bleeding " the brake hydraulic system (expelling the air) is not a routine maintenance operation and should only be necessary when a portion of the hydraulic system has been disconnected or if the level of the fluid has been allowed to fall. The presence of air in the hydraulic system will cause the brakes to feel " spongy ".

During the bleeding operation it is important that the level in the appropriate reservoir is kept topped up to avoid drawing air into the system.

1. Check that all the connections are tightened and all bleed screws closed.

2. Fill the appropriate reservoir with brake fluid of the correct specification.

3. Attach the bleeder tube to the bleed screw on the left-hand rear brake and immerse the open end of the tube in a small quantity of brake fluid contained in a clean glass jar. Slacken the bleed screw and operate the brake pedal slowly backwards and forwards through its full stroke until fluid pumped into the jar is reasonably free from air bubbles. Keep the pedal depressed and close the bleed screw. Release the pedal.

4. Repeat for right-hand rear brake.
   Repeat operation for front brakes.

5. Repeat the complete bleeding sequence until the brake fluid pumped into the jar is completely free from air bubbles.

6. Lock all bleed screws and finally regulate the fluid level in the reservoir.

7. Apply normal working load on the brake pedal for a period of two or three minutes and examine the entire system for leaks.

Do not use the fluid which has been bled through the system to replenish the reservoir as it will have become aerated. Always use fresh fluid straight from the tin. Use only the recommended fluid.

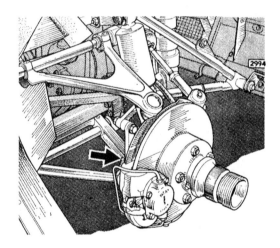

Fig. 91. *Brake bleed nipple (front)*

BLEEDING THE CLUTCH HYDRAULIC SYSTEM
(Not 2+2 Automatic Transmission)

" Bleeding " the clutch hydraulic system (expelling the air) is not a routine maintenance operation and should only be necessary when a portion of the hydraulic system has been disconnected or if the level of the fluid in the reservoir has been allowed to fall. The presence of air in the hydraulic system may result in difficulty in engaging gear owing to the clutch not disengaging fully.

The procedure is as follows :—

Fill up the reservoir with brake fluid exercising great care to prevent the entry of dirt. Attach a rubber bleed tube to the nipple on the slave cylinder on the right-hand side of the clutch housing and allow the tube to hang in a clean glass jar partly filled with brake fluid. Unscrew the nipple one complete turn. Depress the clutch pedal slowly, tighten the bleeder nipple before the pedal reaches the end of its travel and allow the pedal to return unassisted.

Repeat the above procedure, closing the bleed nipple at each stroke, until the fluid issuing from the tube is entirely free of air, care being taken that the reservoir is replenished **frequently** during this operation, for should it be allowed to become empty more air will enter.

On completion, top up the reservoir to the bottom of the filler neck.

Do not on any account use the fluid which has been bled through the system to replenish the reservoir as it will have become aerated. Always use fresh fluid straight from the tin. Use only the recommended fluid.

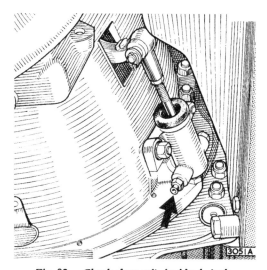

Fig. 92. *Clutch slave cylinder bleed nipple.*

HEADLAMP BEAM SETTING

The alignment of the headlamp beams is set correctly before the car leaves the factory but if for any reason adjustment becomes necessary the following instructions should be carried out.

Place the car on a level surface in front of a garage door or wall ; the car should be at least 25 feet (7.6 m.) away and square to the door or wall. Carry out the work with conditions as dark as possible so that the oval shaped light areas can be seen clearly.

With the headlamps in the full beam positions, that is, not dipped, the beams from the two headlamps should be parallel with the ground and with each other ; measurements should be taken from the centres of the headlamps and the horizontal and vertical axes of the oval light areas.

If adjustment is required remove sealing ring attaching glass lamp shield to wing nacelle and detach shield. Switch on headlamps and check that the beams are not in the dipped position.

The setting of the beams are adjusted by two screws.

The bottom screw ' A ' is for vertical adjustment, that is, to raise or lower the beam ; turn the screw clockwise to lower the beam and anti-clockwise to raise the beam.

The side screw ' B ' is for side adjustment. That is, to turn the beam to right or left. To move the beam to the right turn the screw clockwise. To move the beam to the left turn screw anti-clockwise.

After adjustment replace shield and sealing ring

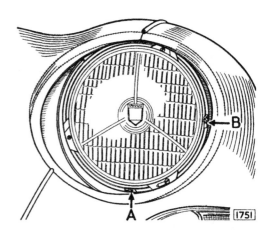

Fig. 93. *Adjustment of the screw ' A ' will alter the headlamp beam in the vertical plane; adjustment of the screw ' B ' will alter the beam in the horizontal plane.*

FUSES

Fuses

Should a component in the electrical system fail to function it is possible that the fuse protecting that component has blown.

Should a replacement fuse of the correct type also blow this indicates a fault in the circuit serving the affected component, and the car should therefore be taken to the nearest Jaguar dealer for examination.

The fuses are located behind the instrument panel and access to them is obtained by removing the two instrument panel retaining screws (top left-hand and right-hand corners). The instrument panel will now hinge downwards exposing fuses and fuse indicator plate.

Circuits controlled by individual fuses are shown on indicator plate and spare fuses are provided. It is essential that a blown fuse is replaced by one of the correct value.

A 35 amp. in-line fuse (20 amp. American rating) is incorporated in the sub-panel of the traffic hazard warning device.

A 15 amp. in-line fuse is incorporated in the circuit of the electrically heated backlight and is located below the fuse block behind the instrument panel.

Always replace spare fuse as soon as possible.

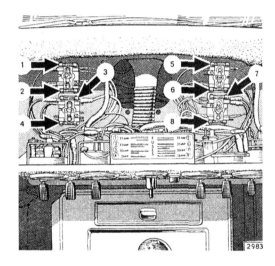

Fig. 94. *Location of fuses.*

	Amps.	Fuse No.
Headlamps		
Main Beam	35	1
Dip Beam	35	2
Horns	50	3
Side, Tail, Panel, Number Plate Lamps	35	5
Horn relay, Washer, Radiator Fan Motor, Stop Lamps	35	6
Flasher, Heater, Wiper, Choke, Fuel, Water, Oil Gauges	35	7
Head Lamp Flash, Interior Lamps, Cigar Lighter	35	8
Electrically heated Backlight (optional extra)	15	—
Traffic hazard warning device (U.S.A. only)	35	—

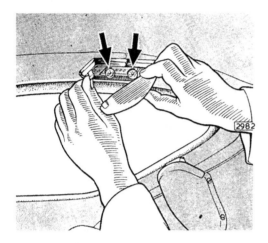

Fig. 99. *Interior lamp bulb removal*
(fixed head coupe)

Rear/Brake Bulb—Replacement

Remove the two screws retaining lamp glass and remove glass. The rear/braking light bulb is the inner one of the two bulbs exposed and is removed by pressing upwards and rotating anti-clockwise. When fitting a replacement bulb note that the pins are offset.

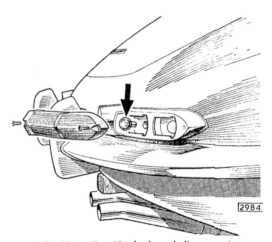

Fig. 101. *Rear/Brake lamp bulb removal.*

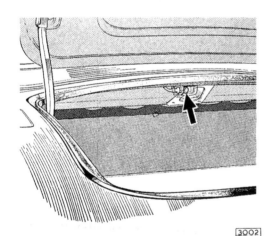

Fig. 100. *Interior lamp bulb removal*
(open 2-seater)

Interior/Luggage Lamp Bulb—Replacement

The Interior/Luggage lamp bulb is retained in a holder accessible when the boot lid is raised. To remove bulb from its holder press in and rotate anti-clockwise.

Number Plate Lamp Bulb—Replacement

Remove fixing screw retaining rim to lamp glass and detach glass and gasket. Remove bulb by pressing and rotating in an anti-clockwise direction.

Traffic Hazard Indicator Bulb—Replacement

Remove the chrome bezel and unscrew the bulb from the bulb holder.

Backlight Heater Indicator Bulb—Replacement

Remove the chrome bezel and unscrew the bulb from the bulb holder.

Reverse Lamp Bulb—Replacement

Remove the two screws retaining the lamp glass and detach the glass and gasket. Remove the bulb by pressing and rotating in an anti-clockwise direction.

Automatic Transmission Indicator Bulb Replacement (2 + 2)

Remove the drive screws and detach the arm rest and transmission unit tunnel cover. Unscrew the gear control knob.

Withdraw two screws and detach the gear indicator cover.

Detach the bulb cover and withdraw the bulb.

Replace the bulb with one of the correct voltage (24 volts).

Fig. 103. *Reverse lamp bulb removal.*

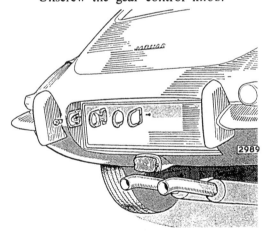

Fig. 102. *Number plate lamp bulb removal.*

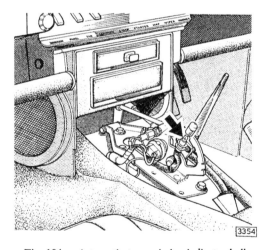

Fig. 104. *Automatic transmission indicator bulb.*

LAMP BULBS—REPLACEMENT

Headlamp Bulb—Replacement

Remove the six screws holding glass headlamp cover retaining ring to wing. Remove ring and rubber seal now exposed.

Remove glass cover.

Release three screws retaining headlamp unit rim and remove rim by turning in an anti-clockwise direction.

Note: It is not necessary to remove screws completely.

Light unit can now be withdrawn.

Remove plug with attached cables from unit. Release bulb retaining spring clips and withdraw bulb.

Replace with bulb of correct type.

When re-assembling note that a groove in the bulb plate must register with a raised portion on the bulb retainer.

Replace spring clip and refit light unit assembly.

Refit retaining ring by turning in a clockwise direction and tighten the three cross head screws.

Note: Do not turn the two slotted screws or the setting of the headlamp will be upset.

Sealed Beam Unit—Replacement

On cars fitted with sealed beam headlights, proceed as described above until the headlight unit is withdrawn.

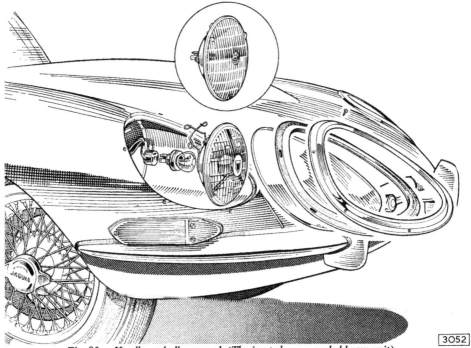

3052

Fig. 95. Headlamp bulb removal. (The inset shows a sealed beam unit).

Sidelamp Bulb—Replacement

Remove three screws retaining lamp glass and remove glass. The side lamp bulb is the inner one of the two exposed and is removed by pressing inwards and rotating anti-clockwise.

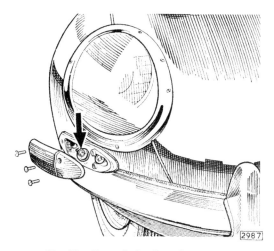

Fig. 97. Front flasher lamp bulb removal.

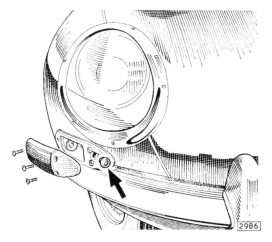

Fig. 96. Sidelamp bulb removal.

Front Flasher Bulb—Replacement

Proceed as for sidelamp bulb. The flasher bulb is the outer one of the two exposed.

Rear Flasher Bulb—Replacement

Proceed as for tail lamp bulb. The flasher bulb is the outer one of the two exposed.

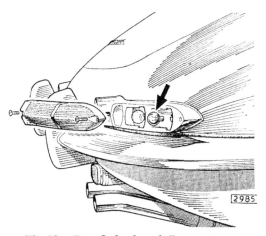

Fig. 98. Rear flasher lamp bulb removal.

CONVERSION TABLES

METRIC INTO ENGLISH MEASURE

1 millimetre is approximately 1/25″, and is exactly ·03937″.
1 centimetre is approximately ⅜″, and is exactly ·3937″.
1 metre is approximately 39⅜″, and is exactly 39·37″ or 1·0936 yards.
1 kilometre is approximately ⅝ mile, and is exactly ·6213 miles.
1 kilogramme is approximately 2¼ lbs., and is exactly 2·21 lbs.
1 litre is approximately 1¾ pints, and is exactly 1·76 pints.
To convert metres to yards, multiply by 70 and divide by 64.
To convert kilometres to miles, multiply by 5 and divide by 8 (approx.).
To convert litres to pints, multiply by 88 and divide by 50.
To convert grammes to ounces, multiply by 20 and divide by 567.
To find the cubical contents of a motor cylinder, square the diameter (or bore), multiply by 0·7854, and multiply the result by the stroke.
1 M.P.G.—0·3546 kilometres per litre or 2.84 litres per kilometre.

MILES INTO KILOMETRES

Kilo.	Miles	Kilo.	Miles	Kilo.	Miles	Kilo.	Miles	Kilo.	Miles
1	⅝	16	10	31	19¼	46	28⅝	60	37¼
2	1¼	17	10⅝	32	19⅞	47	29¼	70	43½
3	1⅞	18	11¼	33	20½	48	29⅞	80	49¾
4	2½	19	11¾	34	21⅛	49	30½	90	55⅞
5	3⅛	20	12⅜	35	21¾	50	31⅛	100	62⅛
6	3¾	21	13	36	22⅜	51	31¾	200	124¼
7	4⅜	22	13⅝	37	23	52	32¼	300	186⅜
8	5	23	14¼	38	23⅝	53	32⅞	400	248½
9	5⅝	24	14⅞	39	24¼	54	33½	500	310¾
10	6¼	25	15½	40	24⅞	55	34⅛	600	372⅞
11	6⅞	26	16⅛	41	25½	56	34¾	700	435
12	7½	27	16¾	42	26⅛	57	35⅜	800	497⅛
13	8⅛	28	17⅜	43	26¾	58	36	900	559¼
14	8¾	29	18	44	27⅜	59	36⅝	1000	621⅜
15	9⅜	30	18⅝	45	28				

PINTS AND GALLONS TO LITRES

Pints	Gallons	Litres Approx.	Litres Exact	Pints	Gallons	Litres Approx.	Litres Exact
1	⅛	½	·57	40	5	23	22·75
2	¼	1	1·14	48	6	27	27·30
3	⅜	1½	1·71	56	7	32	31·85
4	½	2¼	2·27	64	8	36½	36·40
8	1	4½	4·54	72	9	41	40·95
16	2	9	9·10	80	10	45½	45·50
24	3	13½	13·65	88	11	50	50·05
32	4	18	18·20	96	12	54½	54·60

CONVERSION TABLES

RELATIVE VALUE OF MILLIMETRES AND INCHES

mm.	Inches	mm.	Inches	mm.	Inches	mm.	Inches
1	0·0394	26	1·0236	51	2·0079	76	2·9922
2	0·0787	27	1·0630	52	2·0473	77	3·0315
3	0·1181	28	1·1024	53	2·0866	78	3·0709
4	0·1575	29	1·1417	54	2·1260	79	3·1103
5	0·1968	30	1·1811	55	2·1654	80	3·1496
6	0·2362	31	1·2205	56	2·2047	81	3·1890
7	0·2756	32	1·2598	57	2·2441	82	3·2284
8	0·3150	33	1·2992	58	2·2835	83	3·2677
9	0·3543	34	1·3386	59	2·3228	84	3·3071
10	0·3937	35	1·3780	60	2·3622	85	3·3465
11	0·4331	36	1·4173	61	2·4016	86	3·3859
12	0·4724	37	1·4567	62	2·4410	87	3·4252
13	0·5118	38	1·4961	63	2·4803	88	3·4646
14	0·5512	39	1·5354	64	2·5197	89	3·5040
15	0·5906	40	1·5748	65	2·5591	90	3·5433
16	0·6299	41	1·6142	66	2·5984	91	3·5827
17	0·6693	42	1·6536	67	2·6378	92	3·6221
18	0·7087	43	1·6929	68	2·6772	93	3·6614
19	0·7480	44	1·7323	69	2·7166	94	3·7008
20	0·7874	45	1·7717	70	2·7559	95	3·7402
21	0·8268	46	1·8110	71	2·7953	96	3·7796
22	0·8661	47	1·8504	72	2·8347	97	3·8189
23	0·9055	48	1·8898	73	2·8740	98	3·8583
24	0·9449	49	1·9291	74	2·9134	99	3·8977
25	0·9843	50	1·9685	75	2·9528	100	3·9370

RELATIVE VALUE OF INCHES AND MILLIMETRES

Inches	0	$\frac{1}{16}$	$\frac{1}{8}$	$\frac{3}{16}$	$\frac{1}{4}$	$\frac{5}{16}$	$\frac{3}{8}$	$\frac{7}{16}$
0	0·0	1·6	3·2	4·8	6·4	7·9	9·5	11·1
1	25·4	27·0	28·6	30·2	31·7	33·3	34·9	36·5
2	50·8	52·4	54·0	55·6	57·1	58·7	60·3	61·9
3	76·2	77·8	79·4	81·0	82·5	84·1	85·7	87·3
4	101·6	103·2	104·8	106·4	108·0	109·5	111·1	112·7
5	127·0	128·6	130·2	131·8	133·4	134·9	136·5	138·1
6	152·4	154·0	155·6	157·2	158·8	160·3	161·9	163·5
Inches	$\frac{1}{2}$	$\frac{9}{16}$	$\frac{5}{8}$	$\frac{11}{16}$	$\frac{3}{4}$	$\frac{13}{16}$	$\frac{7}{8}$	$\frac{15}{16}$
0	12·7	14·3	15·9	17·5	19·1	20·6	22·2	23·8
1	38·1	39·7	41·3	42·9	44·4	46·0	47·6	49·2
2	63·5	65·1	66·7	68·3	69·8	71·4	73·0	74·6
3	88·9	90·5	92·1	93·7	95·2	96·8	98·4	100·0
4	114·3	115·9	117·5	119·1	120·7	122·2	123·8	125·4
5	139·7	141·3	142·9	144·5	146·1	147·6	149·2	150·8
6	165·1	166·7	168·3	169·9	171·5	173·0	174·6	176·2

ROUTINE MAINTENANCE

Point	Component	MOBIL	CASTROL	SHELL	ESSO	B.P.	DUCK-HAM	REGENT Caltex/Texaco
6	Multigrade engine oils	Mobiloil Special*	Castrol XL 20W/50	Shell Super Oil	Esso Extra Motor Oil 10W/30* Esso Extra Motor Oil 20W/40	Super Visco-Static 10W/40	Q20/50 or Q5500*	Havoline Special 20W/40 or 10W/30*
	Upper cylinder Lubrication	Mobil Upper-lube	Castrollo	Shell U.C.L.or Donax U	Esso U.C.L.	U.C.L.	Adcoid Liquid	Regent U.C.L.
	Distributor oil can points Oil can lubrication ...	Mobiloil A	Castrol XL	Shell X-100 30	Esso Motor Oil 20W/30	Energol SAE 30	NOL 30	Havoline 30
9 15	Rear axle ... ... Gearbox	Mobilube GX 90	Castrol Hypoy	Spirax 90 EP	Esso Gear Oil GP 90/140	Gear Oil SAE 90 EP	Hypoid 90	Multi-Gear Lubricant EP 90
1or10 2&11 7&16 3&12 4&13 8&17	Steering housing ... Front wheel bearings ... Rear wheel bearings ... Distributor cam ... Steering tie-rods ... Wheel swivels ... ... Rear wishbone pivots	Mobil-grease MP	Castrol-grease LM	Retinax A	Esso Multi-purpose grease H	Ener-grease L2	LB 10	Marfak All Purpose
	Automatic transmission unit	Mobil-fluid 200	Castrol T.Q.	Shell Donax T.6	Esso Automatic Trans-mission Fluid	Auto-matic Trans-mission Fluid Type A	Nol-matic	Texa-matic Fluid

*These oils should NOT be used in worn engines requiring overhaul.
If an SAE 30 or 40 oil has previously been used in the engine a slight increase in oil consumption may be noticed but this will be compensated by the advantages gained.

CAPACITIES

	Imperial pints	U.S. pints	Litres
Engine—refill (including filter)	15	18	8.5
Gearbox	2¼	3	1.5
Rear axle	2¾	3¼	1.5
Cooling system (including heater)	32	38.5	18.8
Automatic transmission unit (from dry)	15	18	8.5

	Imperial galls.	U.S. galls.	Litres
Petrol tank	14	16.8	63.6

DRAIN PLUGS

ENGINE

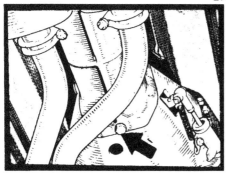

GEARBOX

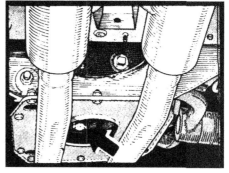

REAR AXLE

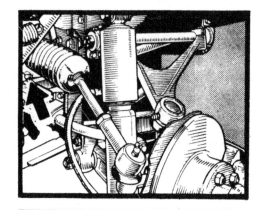

**STEERING HOUSING
(LEFT HAND DRIVE)**

1 ────────────────────

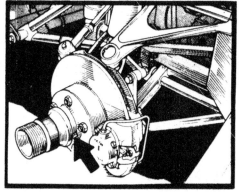

FRONT WHEEL BEARINGS

2 ────────────────────

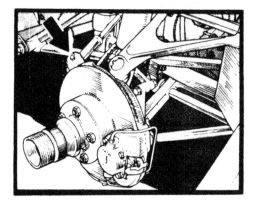

STEERING TIE ROD

3 ────────────────────

WHEEL SWIVELS — 4

BRAKE AND CLUTCH MASTER CYLINDER RESERVOIRS (LEFT HAND DRIVE) — 5

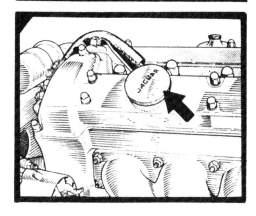

ENGINE OIL FILLER — 6

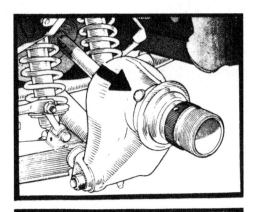

REAR WHEEL BEARINGS ⬛ 7 ─────────

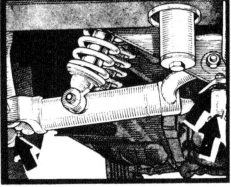

REAR WISHBONE PIVOTS ⬛ 8 ─────────

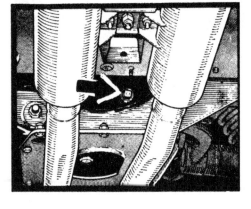

**REAR AXLE LEVEL
AND FILLER PLUG** ⬛ 9 ─────────

**STEERING HOUSING
(RIGHT HAND DRIVE)** ⬤ 10

FRONT WHEEL BEARINGS ⬤ 11

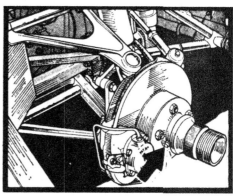

STEERING TIE ROD ⬤ 12

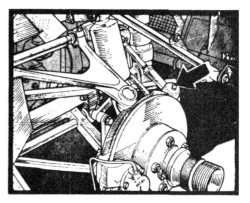

13   WHEEL SWIVELS

BRAKE AND CLUTCH MASTER
CYLINDER RESERVOIRS
(RIGHT HAND DRIVE)

14

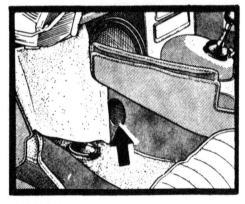

GEARBOX LEVEL AND FILLER
PLUG (MANUAL GEARBOX)

15

REAR WHEEL BEARINGS 16

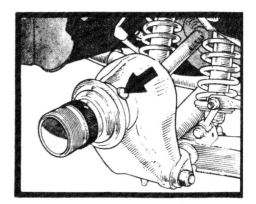

REAR WISHBONE PIVOTS 17

AUTOMATIC TRANSMISSION DIPSTICK 18

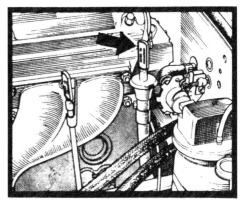

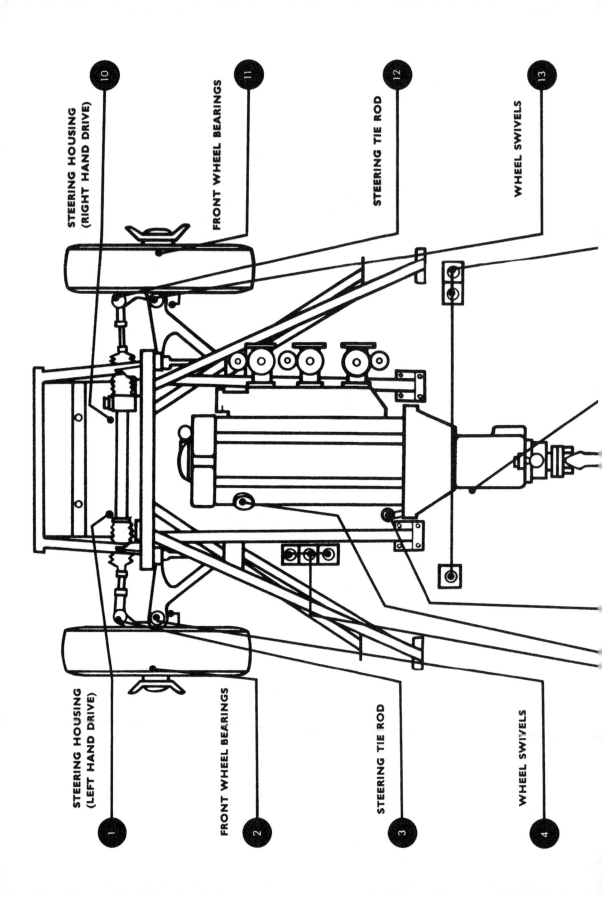

STEERING HOUSING
(RIGHT HAND DRIVE)

FRONT WHEEL BEARINGS

STEERING TIE ROD

WHEEL SWIVELS

10

11

12

13

STEERING HOUSING
(LEFT HAND DRIVE)

FRONT WHEEL BEARINGS

STEERING TIE ROD

WHEEL SWIVELS

1

2

3

4

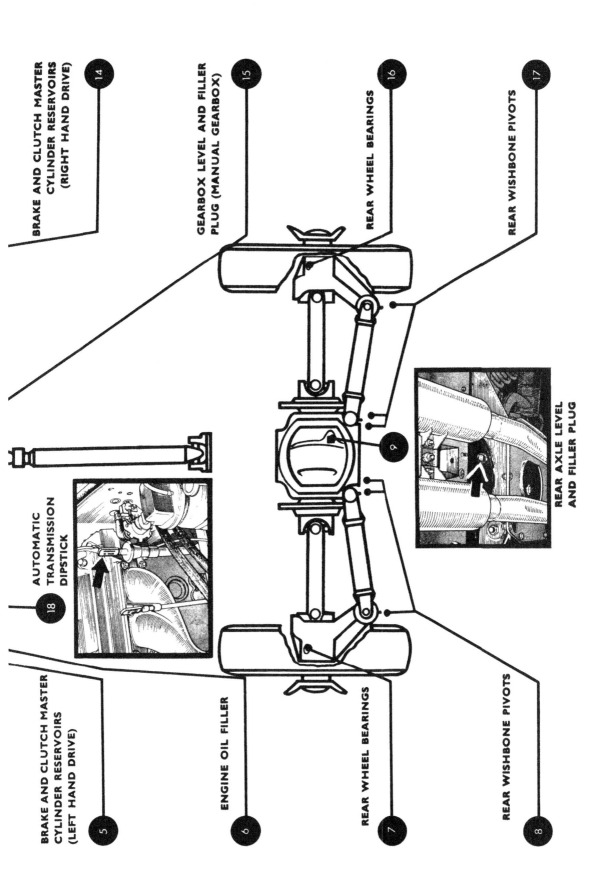

BRAKE AND CLUTCH MASTER CYLINDER RESERVOIRS (RIGHT HAND DRIVE)

14

GEARBOX LEVEL AND FILLER PLUG (MANUAL GEARBOX)

15

REAR WHEEL BEARINGS

16

REAR WISHBONE PIVOTS

17

REAR AXLE LEVEL AND FILLER PLUG

9

AUTOMATIC TRANSMISSION DIPSTICK

18

BRAKE AND CLUTCH MASTER CYLINDER RESERVOIRS (LEFT HAND DRIVE)

5

ENGINE OIL FILLER

6

REAR WHEEL BEARINGS

7

REAR WISHBONE PIVOTS

8

ROUTINE MAINTENANCE

For more detailed information on the periodic maintenance operations listed below see the "Routine Maintenance" section of the Operating, Maintenance and Service Handbook.

Point	
	Daily Check radiator water level Check engine oil level.
	Weekly Check tyre pressures (including spare wheel)
	Monthly Check battery electrolyte level and connections
5 & 14 15—— 9—— 6—— 18——	**Every 3,000 miles (5,000 km)** Check radiator water level Check tyre pressures (including spare wheel) Check battery electrolyte level and connections Check fluid level in brake and clutch master cylinder reservoirs Check gearbox oil level Check rear axle oil level Drain engine sump and refill Renew oil filter element and seal Top up carburetter hydraulic piston dampers Lubricate distributor and check contact points Clean, adjust and test sparking plugs Check carburetter slow running Check fluid level in Automatic Transmission unit (when fitted)
1, 3, 4, 8, 10, 12, 13, 17—	**Every 6,000 miles (10,000 km)** Carry out 3,000 mile (5,000 km) service Lubricate all grease nipples (excluding wheel bearings) Renew oil filter element and seal Clean fuel feed line filter and carburetter filters Examine brake friction pads for wear Clear drain holes in bottoms of doors Adjust top timing chain (if necessary) Check front wheel alignment Check alternator belt for wear Carry out oil can lubrication of (a) seat runner and adjusting mechanism (b) handbrake lever ratchet (c) door locks (d) luggage compartment hinges and lock (e) bonnet hinges and catches (f) windscreen wiper arms (g) accelerator and carburetter linkage (h) fuel filler cover hinge. Tune carburetters
15—— 9—— 2, 7, 11, 16	**Every 12,000 miles (20,000 km)** Carry out 3,000 and 6,000 mile (5,000 and 10,000 km) service Drain and refill gearbox Drain and refill rear axle Renew air cleaner element Renew sparking plugs Lubricate front and rear wheel hub bearings Check front and rear wheel bearings for end-float. (Additional charge for adjustment) Check exhaust system for leaks Check and tighten all chassis and body nuts, bolts and screws Check head lamp alignment
	Every 21,000 miles (35,000 km.) Carry out 3,000 (5,000 km.) service Drain automatic transmission unit : wash out oil pan. Adjust front and rear bands and refill unit.

REAR AXLE—OIL CHANGING

Do NOT drain and refill the rear axle at the first 1,000 miles (1,600 km.) free service. Change the rear axle oil after the car has completed 6,000 miles (10,000 km.) and thereafter at the recommended intervals.

AUTOMATIC TRANSMISSION UNIT

Detailed instructions for "checking the oil level" of the Automatic Transmission unit are contained in the Operating, Maintenance and Service Handbook.

TYRE PRESSURES

Check tyre pressures with the tyres cold, and not when they have attained their normal running temperatures.

Dunlop Road Speed RS5 640 × 15 for speeds up to 130 m.p.h.

Front	Rear
23 lb. per sq. in.	25 lb. per sq. in.
(1.62 kg./sq. cm.)	(1.76 kg./sq. cm.)

For speeds up to maximum or when touring with car fully laden.

30 lb. per sq. in.	35 lb. per sq. in.
(2.11 kg./sq. cm.)	(2.46 kg./sq. cm.)

Dunlop SP.41 H.R. 185 × 15 For speeds up to 125 m.p.h.

32 lb. per sq. in.	32 lb. per sq. in.
(2.25 kg./sq. cm.)	(2.25 kg./sq. cm.)

For speeds up to a maximum or when touring with car fully laden.

40 lb. per sq. in.	40 lb. per sq. in.
(2.81 kg./sq. cm.)	(2.81 kg./sq. cm.)

JAGUAR CARS LIMITED, COVENTRY, ENGLAND

E/131/6

Printed and distributed by Brooklands Books Ltd., PO Box 904, Amersham, Bucks, HP6 9JA, England

Part Number: E/131/6

ISBN 9781869826383   Ref: J36HH   4W4/2993

OFFICIAL TECHNICAL BOOKS

Brooklands Technical Books has been formed to supply owners,
restorers and professional repairers with
official factory literature.

Workshop Manuals

Jaguar Service Manual 1946-1948		9781855207844
Jaguar XK 120 140 150 150S & Mk 7, 8 & 9		9781870642279
Jaguar Mk 2 (2.4 3.4 3.8 240 340)	E121/7	9781870642958
Jaguar Mk 10 (3.8 & 4.2) & 420G	E136/2	9781855200814
Jaguar 'S' Type 3.4 & 3.8	E133/3	9781870642095
Jaguar E-Type 3.8 & 4.2 Series 1 & 2		
	E123/8, E123 B/3 & E156/1	9781855200203
Jaguar E-Type V12 Series 3	E165/3	9781855200012
Jaguar 420	E143/2	9781855201712
Jaguar XJ6 2.8 & 4.2 Series 1		9781855200562
Jaguar XJ6 3.4 & 4.2 Series	E188/4	9781855200302
Jaguar XJ12 Series 1		9781783180417
Jaguar XJ12 Series 2 / DD6 Series 2	E190/4	9781855201408
Jaguar XJ6 & XJ12 Series 3	AKM9006	9781855204010
Jaguar XJ6 OWM (XJ40) 1986-94		9781855207851
Jaguar XJS V12 5.3 & 6.0 Litre	AKM3455	9781855202627
Jaguar XJS 6 Cylinder 3.6 & 4.0 Litre	AKM9063	9781855204638

Owners Workshop Manuals

Jaguar E-Type V12 1971-1974	9781783181162
Jaguar XJ, Sovereign 1968-1982	9781783811179
Jaguar XJ6 Workshop Manual 1986-1994	9781855207851
Jaguar XJ12, XJ5.3 Double Six 1972-1979	9781783181186

Parts Catalogues

Jaguar Mk 2 3.4	J20	9781855201569
Jaguar Mk 2 (3.4, 3.8 & 340)	J34	9781855209084
Jaguar Series 3 12 Cyl. Saloons		9781783180592
Jaguar E-Type 3.8	J30	9781869826314
Jaguar E-Type 4.2 Series 1	J37	9781870642118
Jaguar E-Type Series 2	J37 & J38	9781855201705
Jaguar E-Type V12 Ser. 3 Open 2 Seater	RTC9014	9781869826840
Jaguar XJ6 Series 1		9781855200043
Jaguar XJ6 & Daimler Sovereign Ser. 2	RTC9883CA	9781855200579
Jaguar XJ6 & Daimler Sovereign Ser. 3	RTC9885CF	9781855202771
Jaguar XJ12 Series 2 / DD6 Series 2		9781783180585
Jaguar 2.9 & 3.6 Litre Saloons 1986-89	RTC9893CB	9781855202993
Jaguar XJ-S 3.6 & 5.3 Jan 1987 on	RTC9900CA	9781855204003

Owners Handbooks

Jaguar XK120		9781855200432
Jaguar XK140	E101/2	9781855200401
Jaguar XK150	E111/2	9781855200395
Jaguar Mk 2 (3.4)	E116/10	9781855201682
Jaguar Mk 2 (3.8)	E115/10	9781869826765
Jaguar E-Type (Tuning & prep. for competition)		9781855207905
Jaguar E-Type 3.8 Series 1	E122/7	9781870642927
Jaguar E-Type 4.2 2+2 Series 1	E131/6	9781869826383
Jaguar E-Type 4.2 Series	E154/5	9781869826499
Jaguar E-Type V12 Series 3	E160/2	9781855200029
Jaguar E-Type V12 Series 3 (US)	A181/2	9781855200036
Jaguar XJ (3.4 & 4.2) Series 2	E200/8	9781855201200
Jaguar XJ6C Series 2	E184/1	9781855207875
Jaguar XJ12 Series 3	AKM4181	9781855207868

Carburetters

SU Carburetters Tuning Tips & Techniques	9781855202559
Solex Carburetters Tuning Tips & Techniques	9781855209770
Weber Carburettors Tuning Tips and Techniques	9781855207592

Jaguar - Road Test Books

Jaguar and SS Gold Portfolio 1931-1951	9781855200630
Jaguar XK120 XK140 XK150 Gold Port. 1948-60	9781870642415
Jaguar Mk 7, 8, 9, 10 & 420G	9781855208674
Jaguar Mk 1 & Mk 2 1955-1969	9781855208599
Jaguar E-Type	9781855208360
Jaguar XJ6 1968-79 (Series 1 & 2)	9781855202641
Jaguar XJ12 XJ5.3 V12 Gold Portfolio 1972-1990	9781855200838
Jaguar XJS Gold Portfolio 1975-1988	9781855202719
Jaguar XJ-S V12 1988-1996	9781855204249
Jaguar XK8 & XKR 1996-2005	9781855207578
Road & Track on Jaguar 1950-1960	9780946489695
Road & Track on Jaguar 1968-1974	9780946489374
Road & Track On Jaguar XJ-S-XK8-XK	9781855206298

Available from Jaguar specialists, Amazon and all good motoring bookshops

Brooklands Books Ltd., PO Box 904, Amersham,
Bucks, HP6 9JA, UK

www.brooklandsbooks.com

Printed in Great Britain
by Amazon

58463103R00064